CREATIVE
BASKET MAKING

CREATIVE
BASKET MAKING
Lois Walpole

NORTH
LIGHT
BOOKS

Acknowledgements

This book is mostly all my own work – I wish to make no-one else responsible for any basket makers' faux pas I may have made – but I do want to thank Caroline Churton, the editor, for making a cohesive whole out of the mountain of material she was presented with and for handling the necessary corrections and cuts with supreme skill and discretion.

I want also to thank all the students, past and present, who have forced me to analyse why things are done in certain ways and taught me how best to explain the findings.

Dr John Dransfield at the Royal Botanic Gardens, Kew, very kindly supplied the photograph of rattan growing, and Desmond P. Cody provided an invaluable source of information on the production of cane in a paper for the United Nations Industrial Development Organization (ID/299 1983). The Male family, who grow willows in Somerset, have always been very helpful to me and kindly allowed me to photograph their farm and Hugh stripping willow. Thanks also to Dylon International for providing some dyes for use in the projects.

Finally, thanks to John Brennan; suffice to say that nothing in my life is possible without him.

First published in 1989 in the U.K.
by William Collins Sons & Co., Ltd

First published in the U.S.A., 1989, by
North Light Books, an imprint of
F&W Publications
1507 Dana Avenue
Cincinnati, Ohio 45207
© Lois Walpole 1989

Library of Congress Cataloging-in-Publication Data

Walpole, Lois, *1952–*
   Creative basket making.
   1. Basket making.   I. Title
TT879.B3W35   1989   746.41′2   88-34483
ISBN 0-89134-299-0

Designed by Eve White
Colour photography by Lois Walpole (except for photographs on pp. 3, 8, 13, 112, 115, 140, 147 and 152 by Nigel Cheffers-Heard)
Printed and bound in Italy
by New Interlitho SpA, Milan

This book is dedicated to the memory of Sarah Grosse, artist and craftswoman

Frontispiece: *Large basket randed in white polypropylene tape, with added decoration; height c. 80 cm (31½ in)*
Title page: *Diamond-shaped tray made by the plaiting method*

Contents

Introduction

The origins of the craft

Basket making is thought to be one of the oldest crafts. Evidence of coiled basketwork lining Egyptian pit granaries has been dated to 8000 to 10000 BC. Unfortunately, however, because of the nature of the objects and the materials from which they were made, few ancient baskets have survived, most having either worn out or rotted. Those that have been found have usually been buried in sand or dry earth and mostly in places where the climate is very dry.

Because baskets have been given little status historically (with the exception of ceremonial or burial pieces), few cultures have made any attempt to preserve old examples. It was only in the eighteenth century, with the arrival of Europeans on the North American continent, that collections of native Indian basketry began to be made. As a result there are few places where the aspiring basket maker of today can go to study examples from the past. In Britain the Museum of English Rural Life at Reading University has a collection of mainly nineteenth- and early twentieth-century baskets and in North America there are several museums with collections of Indian baskets. There are a few collections in Europe, but even the bigger ones are nowhere near the size of those of antique ceramics, for example, to be found in major museums around the world.

However, because basketry has been practised continuously in some form or another in most regions, the same techniques that were used centuries ago can still be found in contemporary baskets being made throughout the world. I doubt if it is possible for anyone to invent a weave or technique that has not been used a thousand times before, yet there is always scope for individuality through the choice of materials, colours and techniques.

How different techniques were born

Traditionally, basket makers used the materials that were available in their environment. So, if they lived in desert regions they used scrub materials and earth dyes; if they lived in densely forested areas they used either bark or split wood. In temperate climates basket makers used the

straight twigs of deciduous trees and the reeds growing in rivers and lakes, while in tropical areas bamboo and all the varieties of cane were the most readily available materials. Naturally, different techniques evolved to deal with different types of material. Fine coiled or twined baskets were made in those places where the materials themselves were fine and short in length, and robust woven baskets were made where twig-type material was more common. In areas where the local material lent itself to splitting into regular flat strips – such as large leaves, rattans and straight saplings – a plaited form of basket making developed.

As people settled in other countries so they took their skills with them. Thus, when the Europeans and Scandinavians first emigrated to North America and found similar materials to those they had used in their home countries, they introduced there a European way of basket making which quickly developed into its own style, as dictated by the variations in local materials. An example of this is Appalachian basketry.

Baskets used to be made either to perform a specific function – for example, trapping, carrying or storing – or to be used in a spiritual context as a ceremonial item, such as the sacred Navajo baskets of North America which were used for healing and marriage rituals. Nowadays, with the invention of plastics and cardboards and their subsequent use for items such as fishing nets, carrier bags and food cartons, in industrialized countries the practical necessity for most baskets is not so great. Yet we do still seem to have an emotional need for baskets in that we like the look and feel of them, and many of us buy and use baskets even though their synthetic equivalents might be more efficient and practical.

With the widening of world trade in the twentieth century and the importing of products from countries where labour costs are lower, the European basket maker has been unable to compete on price terms; those workshops that have survived in Europe have done so either by keeping their wages as low as possible or by making much of the fact that what they create is an indigenous product. There are dark mutterings amongst British basket makers about the imported basketware from the Far East being inferior in quality, but in fact most of this basketry exported to Europe and North America is intricate and highly skilled work, which is being sold at very low prices.

As we have been able to import baskets so we have also been able to import raw materials.

7

Those of us wanting to make baskets can now choose to use materials grown on the other side of the world, and often it may be as easy to obtain them as it is a product grown in one's own country. In a way this is a pity because the homogeneity of materials and techniques that comes from using indigenous materials is being lost; but on the other hand it would be ridiculous not to use imported materials just because they are imported. Rather we should appreciate that so much material is available to us and take advantage of the fact, at the same time being aware always of where the materials and techniques that we use have come from before adopting them as our own.

The indigenous approach can be extremely successful if followed assiduously. A fine example of a British craftsman who works in this way is David Drew, whose beautiful baskets, made from willows that he has grown and harvested himself in Somerset, tell a story of the maker and his environment with an honesty and purity that would be lost if he made those same baskets in an urban environment.

My baskets

My own approach to basket making has to some extent come out of my environment. Whilst not actually thinking about the 'indigenous approach' at the time, I was aware when I started making baskets that ones made solely of willow would be an inappropriate product to come from the East End of London (where I live and work) in the late twentieth century. My way of designing, which for reasons of economy has always been to use the available material as a starting point for choosing suitable form and technique, has resulted in a style that says something about me and where I live.

It is very easy for me to purchase cane, because I can phone an order to the cane supplier and have the material delivered a few days later. But on the way to visit my parents in Devon I drive past the willow growing area so I also collect willow en route. In addition, as someone who has always been astonished by the things that people throw out into skips, or just onto the streets, it was a natural progression for me to collect and use in my baskets any such materials that were suitable – cables, netting, plastic tape, cardboard, and plastic in all its forms – trying to combine them in an appropriate way. Therefore I use willow for structure and strength, cane for woven patterns and colour, cardboard for painting on and infilling, and plastic tape for colour and washability.

The techniques that I use are mainly the traditional European stake and strand methods, with the addition of the more universal plaiting. I seldom use coiling or soft twining because these

8

techniques are both very labour-intensive and unsuited to the fairly large scale on which I usually work; but I would not deliberately avoid them if they seemed appropriate for the materials in hand.

Designing your baskets

It seems to me that there are only three valid reasons for making a basket that is exactly the same as someone else's: for the purpose of learning the technique by imitation, or because the basket's function demands a specific design that cannot be altered, or because you are being paid to do just that! Having said that, however, I believe it is very important that wherever possible you should make your baskets as original and individual as you can – otherwise you might just as well go out and buy a ready-made one.

This can be achieved in many ways: maybe by using materials that you have grown in your own garden; maybe by using your favourite colours, or the colours that fit in with a room at home. You could make a basket to mark a special occasion – a celebratory basket – perhaps for the birth of a child, or for a wedding, for example.

There is a very direct line between basket making and your personality, more so than with some other crafts, because no tools or machines are used which might interfere in the transfer of ideas from the brain to the hand. Your basketry can therefore become the means of expressing your personality in a visual way. Of course, to be able to do this successfully you need to have a thorough knowledge of the basic methods and techniques of basket making and must learn how to use those skills creatively. The learning process is continuous and the more you learn about the different techniques available, the more likely it is that you will be able to express yourself fully.

It is the combination of idea and skill in execution that makes a good basket; one without the other is seldom satisfactory. A well-made basket lacking imagination is dull, and a badly made basket with an exciting concept is disappointing. This is as true of the humble bread basket as the 'art' basket.

Practical skill does not come easily; it has to be worked at. I am still working at it and I make no pretence that if you follow the instructions in this book you will instantly make beautiful baskets, but I hope they will provide a knowledge of basic skills with which you can go forth and practise.

Sources of inspiration

Inspiration does not come out of thin air; it comes from the store of information each person carries

Left: *Lois Walpole at work in her studio*

around with him or her that is based on things seen, heard, read or otherwise absorbed. Any of it can be drawn on as a basis for design, as long as you allow yourself to consider anything and everything as fair game for inspiration. It may be the texture, the colour, or the shape of something that draws your attention; all that matters is that there is some aspect that is of strong interest to you, even if you cannot see its potential as a starting point for the design of a basket at the time. You can deliberately file these thoughts or observations into your memory for future use, and a sketch or a photograph can act as the key to open up the memory when you want to use the

filed item. This becomes an almost unconscious process for anyone who has had any art training. Those who have not must learn to develop this technique, like any other skill, by practice.

The idea that you start with may be tiny – perhaps just a colour that you have seen and liked. To develop the idea you must work through a mental elimination process, visualizing the colour, say, in big or small areas, with other colours or not. Then, in your mind, you should try out shapes and materials. When you are just starting to develop your design skills you can help yourself enormously by working through this process in a sketchbook, so that you have a record of it. Some of the ideas that you have eliminated for one particular project may come in handy later for another one, so a permanent source of reference like this can be very useful.

Designing the basket is for me the most interesting and exciting part of the whole process. Some of the things that I have used as inspiration seemed very unlikely at the time – such as a yellow crash barrier seen against a blue sea with white rocky islands in the background. Several years later I turned the crash barrier into a yellow spiral that disappeared into the bottom of a blue cane bowl. I often use other basket and ceramic shapes I have seen as a starting point for my own designs, and when I paint on card I use as inspiration anything from paintings by Picasso to ski-maps.

About this book

Because I believe that it is possible to explain practical things only if one's knowledge is empirical, I have restricted myself in this book to the two distinct categories of basket making – stake and strand, and plaiting – that I use in my own work. The first part of the book features stake and strand methods and the second concentrates on plaiting, but each section is self-contained in that it is not necessary to learn one technique before the other. At the end of each section I have included a number of projects, which I offer to you as learning exercises in techniques or as springboards for your own ideas.

I have tried to create the sort of book that would have been useful to me when I started learning basket making and that I could have used later as a visual stimulus while teaching at adult institutes and day centres, where the environment has often been less than conducive to exciting ideas. I hope also that it will appeal to those who already make baskets but who, like me, are always looking for new ways to go about things.

In Britain there is a growing awareness (already established in the United States) among people involved in textile crafts of the close relationship between many basketry and textile disciplines: they, too, may find something of interest in this book. Whatever your level of skill or craft interest, however, I hope above all that this book will inspire you to have a go at making your own baskets.

Left: *Fruit bowl made of polypropylene tape and plastic cane; diameter c. 50 cm (19¾ in)*

STAKE AND STRAND METHOD

Stake and strand basketry is found in many parts of the world. It is probably most highly developed in Europe where willow is the predominant material and in Asia where bamboo and rattan are the most common.

The term 'stake and strand' describes the technique that uses uprights (stakes), which are usually quite widely spaced, and weavers (strands), which lie closely one upon another. Generally it requires that the uprights are stronger than the weavers.

The variations in technique within the stake and strand method are due to the materials, which all have individual characteristics that determine the way they are worked. Willows, for instance, taper, have a finite length, and do not like to be bent too sharply without assistance, therefore the techniques for willow have evolved around these qualities. An example of this is French randing (see page 25), which cleverly creates an even-graded texture out of tapering material. This weave is generally superfluous when working in bamboo or centre cane because the material is a regular width and comes in long lengths, making it possible therefore to weave an even texture just by randing with a single weaver (although French randing is very useful in coloured work).

Right: *Selection of baskets made by the stake and strand method*

In this section I have tried to outline as clearly as possible some of the various weaves, borders, methods of construction, and finishing touches for different-shaped baskets in centre cane or peeled willow. I also explain what materials are required and how to prepare them, and describe some of the tools and equipment you will need for your basket making. Where techniques differ according to whether you are working with cane or willow these are pointed out. All the techniques are equally appropriate, perhaps with small adaptations, for many other materials.

This is a section to dip into as you need it. It does not require that you work through it all before you attempt one of the projects included at the end of it, because within each project you will be referred to the relevant techniques should you need to look them up: words or phrases in *italics* indicate that the subject is dealt with more fully elsewhere, easily located by referring to the index.

Materials

The two materials that I use most in stake and strand basketry are cane and willow.

Cane

Cane is the stem of the climbing palm known generally as rattan. The genus most commonly used for basketry material is *Calamus* and within this genus some 370 species are to be found growing in the area from West Africa to Fiji and Southern China to Queensland, the greatest concentration being in Southeast Asia.

When *Calamus* is harvested it consists of a long climbing stem with a cluster of palm-type leaves at the top and prickly leaf sheaths which it uses to climb with. Rattans produce a small, edible fruit, sometimes as many as a thousand on a single stem. In height they can grow up to 200 m (656 ft) although most commonly they are about 20 m (66 ft) tall.

The cane is harvested by hand when it is eight to twelve years old and the outer thorny leaf sheaths are scraped or cut off. The lengths of cane are then carried on foot to a depot where they are cut to manageable lengths of between 2 m (6½ ft) and 9 m (29½ ft), depending on the cane's intended use and the country in which it is harvested.

Before it reaches us the cane has undergone many treatments, which means that whilst it is a natural product it has nevertheless been processed to make it easy to use – rather in the same way that wool and cotton are produced. The preliminary stages of processing vary considerably in different countries and include killing insects on the plant; removing the shiny outer silicate layer; buffing the surface to make it more attractive; fumigating it to improve the colour; or boiling it in oil to strengthen it by removing resins. The canes are then dried and poles that are to be turned into centre cane are further processed by exporters, who split off the outer skin to make chair cane and turn the inner core into round- and flat-section centre cane (flat-band or lapping cane).

The main enemy of the rattan processor is fungus and the staining and blemishing that this causes. The spores travel fast up the capillary-like structure of the rattan poles and for this reason many of the processes are done within as short a time as possible after harvesting, so as to get the material dry quickly and thereby inhibit growth.

Indonesia is the dominant supplier of raw rattan, providing some 90 per cent of the world's requirements. Hong Kong and Singapore are the main processors and Italy, Taiwan and the United States the biggest importers. It is in the interest of developing countries (where the material is grown and the labour cheap) to turn the raw material into finished goods, such as baskets and furniture, which can then be sold to the West for a much higher price than the raw material. As a result the Philippines and Malaysia have started to levy high export taxes in an attempt to limit the export of raw materials, and Indonesia has introduced an outright ban on the export of raw cane.

Sizing and quality

When the centre core is cut it is milled to various widths which start at a fraction of a millimetre and increase to 8 mm (5/16 in). The resulting round-section canes are graded Very Very Fine 000, Very Fine 00, Fine 0, then Nos. 1–16. The larger canes are known as handle cane, which is available in sizes between 8 mm (5/16 in) and 12 mm (1/2 in). The 8 mm (5/16 in) handle cane is also sometimes labelled as No. 20.

The table below lists the different sizes of centre cane available and may be used as a general guide. However, this method of grading cane is unfortu-

CANE SIZES

Metric	No. (British)	No. (American)
1.375 mm	000	–
1.5 mm	00	1
1.625 mm	0	–
1.75 mm	1	2
1.875 mm	2	–
2 mm	3	2½
2.25 mm	4	3
2.5 mm	5	3½
2.625 mm	6	–
2.75 mm	7	4
3 mm	8	–
3.25 mm	9	4½
3.375 mm	10	–
3.5 mm	11	5
3.75 mm	12	–
4 mm	13	5½
4.25 mm	14	–
4.5 mm	15	6
5 mm	16	7
5.5 mm	–	7½
6 mm	–	8
6.5 mm	–	8½
7 mm	–	9
7.5 mm	–	9½
8 mm	20	10

Left: A rattan (Calamus ovoideus) growing wild in the rain forests of Sri Lanka (photo: J. Dransfield)

nately not consistent. A No. 2 seems to mean different things to different processors so I have found it easier to ignore numbers (the labels always fall off anyway) and have learned to go by eye and feel, and the needs of the job in hand. If you are using willow you will find in a bolt of a particular length individual rods in an enormous range of widths and you just have to learn to judge what is right, so you might as well do the same with cane. Having said that, I have in fact specified widths and numbers in the projects in this book, but they can always be varied by a number in each direction and are intended only as a guide for those who have not yet learned to 'feel' for the right size.

Cane also comes in different qualities, the most commonly available in Britain being Far Eastern Red Tie, Continental Green Label, Blue Tie and Bleached. Generally the Continental Green Label and Blue Tie are the best quality and the Red Tie and Bleached poorer, but I use mainly Red Tie and find it good enough for my purposes although it is 'hairier' than the others. It is usually necessary to go for a better-quality cane to get the small sizes, probably because it is just not possible to split poor-quality cane very finely. The bleached cane can have a spaghetti-like quality that makes it very brittle when dry but incredibly pliable when wet, which could be useful when working a lot of packing where the cane has to make many U-bends. Whenever I have used the better-quality canes I have found them less pliable than the Red Tie, but it is possible I have just been unlucky. There is no getting away from the fact that within each type of cane there will be some that is very pliable and some that just will not bend without cracking.

Buying and storing cane

In Britain cane is bought by the 0.5 kg hank and in North America it seems to be by the pound, but whichever weight is used, try not to buy it coiled up. It may be easier to pack and post in that way, but it creates problems when you want to use it. If the cane has been coiled, you will find that when you want to cut long stakes you will end up with something that resembles a spring. It is then impossible to control the shape of the basket. I try to buy cane in sufficient quantities that it is sent to me like a carpet in a long roll, and then I store it by hanging it from a peg high on the wall. Even a long oval shape is better than coils, so badger your supplier not to coil the material.

Cane will become brittle if stored in a centrally heated or very dry atmosphere for too long. It is best kept in a dry, cool place away from direct sunlight, and it can keep for several years in the right conditions.

Willow

I am referring here to the varieties of *Salix* grown in Europe specifically for basket making. There are also many species of willow not grown for basket making that are suitable for use as well, as long as they are prepared in the right manner. These are not covered in this book, however, because I am not familiar with them, having used what is often referred to as 'hedgerow' material on only a few occasions.

Most of the willow grown in Britain for basket making comes from the Somerset Levels, a triangle of land bordered by the rivers Parrett, Tone and Yeo. Small amounts of willow are also grown in East Anglia and the Nottingham area. The Somerset Levels are flat and fertile, dotted with attractive villages and ancient pubs. Many of the farms there are involved in growing willows and there are quite a few resident basket makers. The species of willow grown is mainly *Salix Triandra* of the variety Black Maul, which produces straight rods up to 2 m (6½ ft) in length. The plant has almond-shaped leaves of a silvery green colour. *Salix Triandra* has, I understand, been difficult to obtain on the North American continent, but I gather the situation is now improving. However, there are many other varieties of willow that will serve the purpose, though they will undoubtedly be harder to prepare and use than a material that is grown and prepared specifically for the purpose of making baskets.

Basket willows are grown commercially like any other crop. They are planted in rows and on the bigger farms harvested mechanically. The first harvest is in the third year, the first two years having been spent nurturing the new plants and defending them from weeds, insects, fungi and frost. The willow beds can then go on being harvested for up to fifty years.

Whether rods are harvested by hand or machine they must then be sorted into lengths. Some of the crop will be dried with its bark on and sold as 'brown' willow; some is boiled and then peeled, the tannin in the bark penetrating the wood and colouring it a golden brown colour, and this is known as 'buff' willow. The remainder of the crop will be stood over winter in a few centimetres of water and then when the sap rises the following spring the bark can be easily peeled, leaving a creamy white rod; this is called 'white'

willow. Willows used to be stripped by hand but most of the process is now done by a machine which flays the bark off and looks as though it might flay a few fingers off as well! When the stripped willows are thoroughly dry they are made into bolts, which are tied using two rods and a decorative knot known as a bond.

A willow rod has its own anatomy: the butt is at the bottom and is the widest part; the belly is the concave side; the back is the convex side; and the tip is at the top and is the finest part.

Left: *Bolts of brown willow*

Centre: *Brown willow drying in the orchard*

Right: *Stripping willow rods*

Sizing and quality

The standard measurement of willow is a bolt. The circumference of a bolt of willow 5 cm (2 in) from the bottom should be 94 cm (37 in) and bolts are sold by the foot length, usually from 3 ft to 8 ft (1 m to 2.5 m). (For this reason, imperial measurements are used when referring to willow rods, although metric equivalents are also provided.) Unlike cane, there is no standard for grading the quality of willow and it seems to vary quite a lot. Ideally there should be no branching of the rod and no knots, and the bark should be completely peeled on buff and white willow. I have come across some willow that will not bend sharply without cracking no matter how it is prepared or dealt with, but unfortunately there really is no way of telling beforehand by looking at the bolt whether it is going to be troublesome.

Buying and storing willow

Bolts are usually sold complete at a standard price for each type regardless of length, the white being more expensive and the brown the cheapest. I have always thought this method of pricing was odd because you get far more weight, though fewer rods, in an 8 ft (2.5 m) bolt than a 3 ft (1 m) one, but I expect there is a good reason for it.

Willow should be stored in as dry, cool, airy and dark a place as possible. Central heating makes it brittle, damp makes it mouldy, and sunlight darkens white willow. Keep the willow tied in its bolts and take it out as needed from the bottom of the bolt. As the bolt loosens, move the top tie down to keep it together.

Tools and Equipment

The tools and equipment required for stake and strand basketry are relatively simple and inexpensive to buy. The essentials for cane and willow differ slightly:

Cane
Knife
Secateurs
Side-cutters
Round-nosed pliers
Small-sized bodkin
    or awl
Medium-sized bodkin
    or awl
Flexible steel tape
    measure
Sink or trough
Screwblock
Weights

Willow
Knife
Secateurs
Medium-sized bodkin
    or awl
Large-sized bodkin
    or awl
Rapping iron
Flexible steel tape
    measure
Sink or trough
Screwblock
Weights

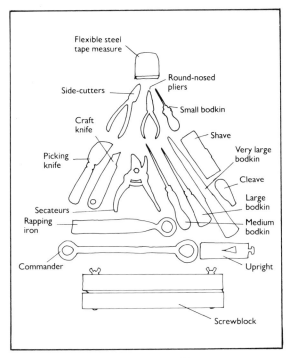

Left: Tools required for the stake and strand method

medium one a diameter of 6–12 mm (¼–½ in); and a large one a diameter of 20 mm (¾ in) or more.

Rapping iron: A rapping iron is a heavy piece of metal usually narrower at one end and often having a ring built in at that end which is used as a commander (see below). It is used mainly in willow work and is for beating the work into order, knocking stakes in, levelling the top edge, cramming off (see page 66), etc.

Flexible steel tape measure: The retractable type is most convenient and is particularly useful because it can be used both as a rigid measure or to measure around the curve of a basket – for the positioning of handles, for example.

Sink or trough: This is used for soaking material in and needs to be of a reasonable size for willow.

Screwblock: This consists of two pieces of wood held together by two bolts which can be adjusted to hold sticks in place when making a square or rectangular base. It is fairly simple to make your own screwblock, but the same end can be achieved by using two pieces of wood and a couple of G-clamps. The wood should be heavy enough not to bow when tightened. The screwblock should sit solidly on your work surface and should be long enough to work as wide a base as you may need.

Weights: These are used to put into the basket whilst you are working up the sides. They hold the basket down on the work surface and leave your hands free to concentrate on the actual weaving. Anything fairly heavy and stable will do. I use plastic tubs filled with rocks for big baskets and a small slab of iron (in a plastic bag because it can rust) for small cane baskets.

In addition to these items there are a few other pieces of equipment which can be useful when working with willow.

Commander: This is a piece of metal either with a ring at each end or with a U-shaped hook at one end and a ring at the other. It is used to straighten willow rods by pulling them through the ring or hook against the curve.

Skeining tools: These are used for making flat skeins out of willow and comprise a *cleave*, for splitting the rod into three parts lengthways; a *shave*, for removing the pith; and an *upright*, for making the skeins a regular width. Skeins can be used to wrap handles with or even to weave the entire basket.

Picking knife: This is a curved-bladed knife used to pick the ends off in willow work – I am told it is invaluable once you have mastered the art of using it, but I haven't yet!

Knives: Craft knives are suitable for most purposes. These should have blades that can be replaced or sharpened effectively because a sharp blade is essential. The handle of the knife should be comfortable and large enough for you to be able to grip using your whole hand. Knives designed specifically for willow work (picking knives) can be bought from specialist suppliers in Britain and craft shops in America.

Secateurs: These are used for cutting willows and the larger sizes of cane. They should be the kind that have a shear action as opposed to the anvil type, which have a tendency to crush willow.

Side-cutters: These are used for most cutting jobs in canework and particularly for trimming ends. Choose ones with as pointed a nose as possible for getting into small spaces and close to the work.

Round-nosed pliers: These are used for squeezing canes at the upsett (see page 49) and at borders; the squeezing action enables the cane to bend without cracking. Choose pliers with a nose that is round and smooth, not D-shaped, and preferably at least 4–6 cm (1½–2½ in) in length.

Bodkins or awls: A bodkin was a weapon in Shakespeare's time. Made of mild steel with a wooden handle, it is long and pointed and is very useful for basket making. Bodkins come in various sizes and are good for splitting sticks and creating spaces where required. A small bodkin has a diameter of 3 mm (⅛ in) at the stock; a

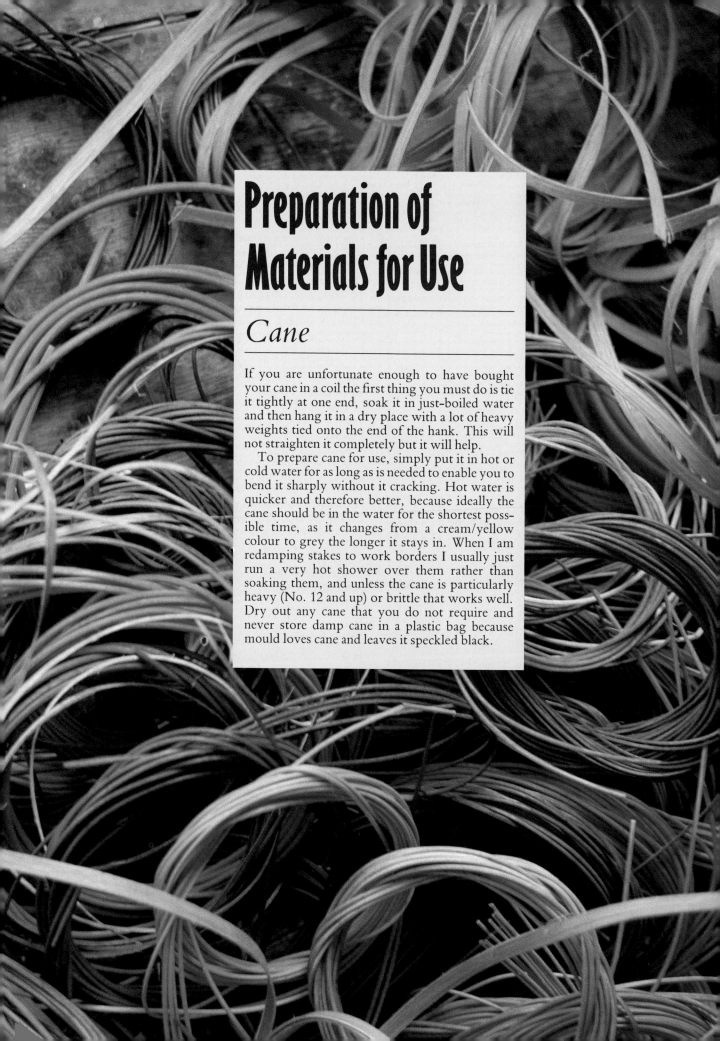

Preparation of Materials for Use

Cane

If you are unfortunate enough to have bought your cane in a coil the first thing you must do is tie it tightly at one end, soak it in just-boiled water and then hang it in a dry place with a lot of heavy weights tied onto the end of the hank. This will not straighten it completely but it will help.

To prepare cane for use, simply put it in hot or cold water for as long as is needed to enable you to bend it sharply without it cracking. Hot water is quicker and therefore better, because ideally the cane should be in the water for the shortest possible time, as it changes from a cream/yellow colour to grey the longer it stays in. When I am redamping stakes to work borders I usually just run a very hot shower over them rather than soaking them, and unless the cane is particularly heavy (No. 12 and up) or brittle that works well. Dry out any cane that you do not require and never store damp cane in a plastic bag because mould loves cane and leaves it speckled black.

Dyeing cane

If I had not found out how simple it is to dye cane I doubt very much if I would still be making baskets. Using coloured cane provides many additional possibilities and can give great variety to your work. Because centre cane is the pith of the plant, it is very absorbent and is therefore an ideal material to dye. For me the criteria for choosing the type of dye have always been ease of use (preferably requiring no boiling) and as little in the way of measuring out extra additives as possible. For this reason I have always used multi-purpose fabric dyes, which require only a bucket, plastic gloves, a kettle and salt. Fibre-reactive dyes are generally considered to be the safest dyes for home and school use and are produced under many different brand names. There are also other types of dye that work equally well, though the process may be more time-consuming.

If you are using a bucket, obviously you will have to separate the cane and wind it into loose coils of just four or five strands to leave room for the dye to circulate freely. It is possible to dye stakes straight if you use a plastic trough or window box.

To prepare a multi-purpose dye solution, put the contents of one tin of dye and one tablespoon of salt into a plastic bucket and pour on at least two kettlefuls of just-boiled water. Put in the cane and leave until it is the colour you want. As the mixture cools you will find it is necessary to leave the cane in longer. Soaking cane in dye for a long time does not seem to affect it adversely in the way that leaving it in water does and occasionally I leave cane in overnight. Some colours keep going longer than others – I have always found turquoise to be one of those. I tend to run out of material to dye before it is exhausted, so I use a lot of turquoise, one of my favourite colours.

Once the cane is the required colour, take it out of the bucket and drain it on newspaper. When it is no longer dripping I put it on a rack over a radiator or in a warm place to dry it as quickly as possible. The instructions that come with the dye suggest the material should be rinsed immediately, but I think that drying it first has the effect of helping to bake in the colours a bit better. I rinse the cane just prior to using it and find that less colour seems to come out at this stage. When working with dyed cane I always wipe the dampened cane with an old towel before weaving it, to take off any loose colour that otherwise goes all over your hands and smudges into the other colours you are using. This is particularly annoying if you are using dyed cane in conjunction with natural cane.

Left: Dyed cane

Willow

Willow also has to be soaked before use and you will not get away with much less than half an hour in hot water, or an hour in cold water for small rods. Hot water is unorthodox but does speed things up. Heavier rods (6 ft/1.80 m and up) will need to be left in cold water for up to three hours (but again, less in hot). Because the willow cannot be bent when it is dry you have to soak it full-length, ideally in a trough. I have always managed up to 8 ft (2.5 m) rods in a standard bath by soaking and wrapping the tips first and then soaking the butts. This method works as long as you do not need to have a bath for a few hours! Weight the rods down in the water so that they are completely immersed.

After soaking, drain the water and cover the willow with a wet cloth – an old blanket or towel will do – and leave it for at least as long as the soaking. This process, called mellowing, lets the water work into the rod whilst at the same time drying the outer surface sufficiently to make it pleasant to handle. If left too long, however, the rods start to develop a mould which gives them a greasy feel and they will then need to be washed before you can use them.

When you come to use the willow you will find that small rods dry out very quickly, especially if you are working in a centrally heated place. The ideal conditions for working willow are like those found in the caves in the Touraine region of France – damp, dark and cold; but we do not have to be martyrs to our craft so just make sure that you keep the rods you are not using under the mellowing blanket and accept that you may need to soak the whole basket before you can put the border down. Personally, I love to work out of doors but most of the time the sun and wind make it impossible with this type of basketry.

Dyeing willow

This is not something I have done very much because it is not as easy as dyeing cane, although the basic procedure is the same. The willow has to be left straight so you need a long trough or some other similar container to dye it in. The same dyes that are suitable for cane can be used, and I have it on good authority from John Galloway, a contemporary British basket maker who makes beautiful dyed willow baskets, that Procion dyes work particularly well.

WARNING: Most dyes are poisonous. They can be taken in through the lungs and skin and are to a greater or lesser extent thought to be carcinogenic, so take great care when using them. Always wear gloves and a protective face mask; do not inhale the powder; and do not stand over a steaming bucket of dye breathing in the vapours.

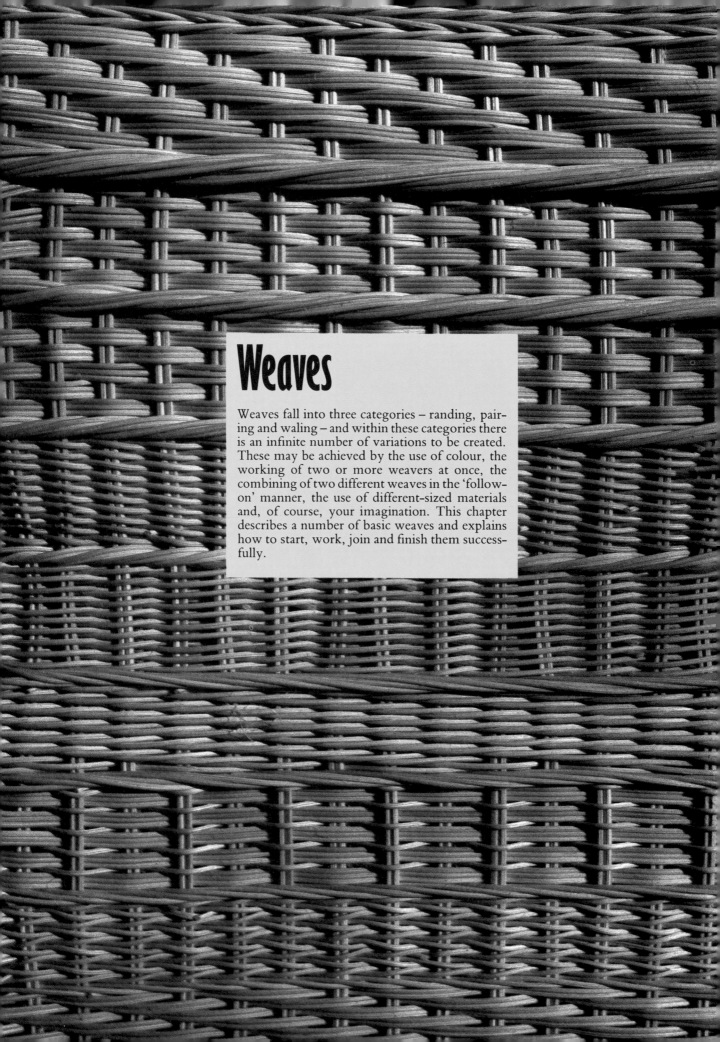

Weaves

Weaves fall into three categories – randing, pair-ing and waling – and within these categories there is an infinite number of variations to be created. These may be achieved by the use of colour, the working of two or more weavers at once, the combining of two different weaves in the 'follow-on' manner, the use of different-sized materials and, of course, your imagination. This chapter describes a number of basic weaves and explains how to start, work, join and finish them success-fully.

Randing Weaves

Randing

This is the simple weave that is the foundation of all weaving: a single strand snaking in and out of uprights. It requires an odd number of stakes. The word could possibly have come from Old English, in which 'rand' meant a border, although a more recent definition of the word is 'a strip', particularly of leather. In basketry the term is usually associated with willow work and there are many variations of the basic randing weave.

How it is done: Take a single weaver and work it alternately in front of and behind the stakes. Continue in this manner.

Joins: The type of join to choose depends on the material being used, the position of the join in the basket, and the degree of strength required. In willow, joins are generally made butt to butt and tip to tip, but sometimes a butt is joined to a tip, as in slewing (see page 26). You could try both methods and use whichever seems appropriate and looks best.

Laid-behind join: This join requires very careful trimming but looks neat on the front. It is often used for square bases in willow. Both ends are left behind the same stake.

Laid-behind join

Several rows of randing

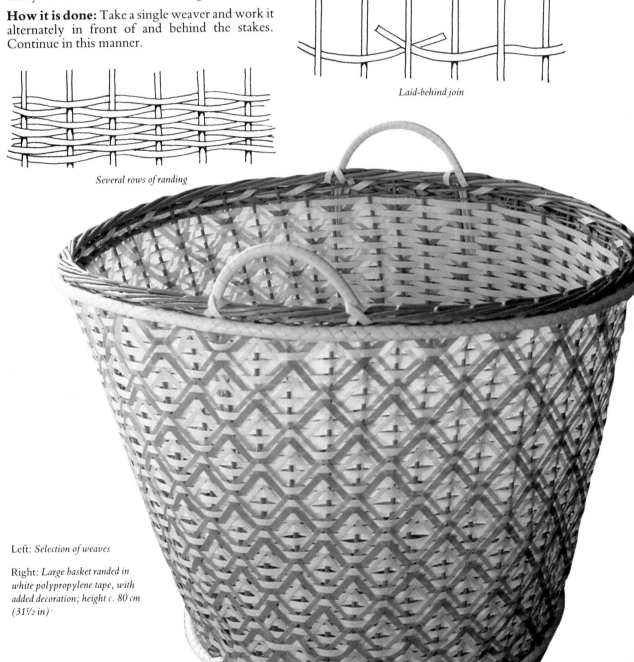

Left: *Selection of weaves*

Right: *Large basket randed in white polypropylene tape, with added decoration; height c. 80 cm (31½ in)*

Crossed-over join: This is a strong and neat join. The old end is brought to the front and the new end pushed into the work under and to the left of it. Each end is trimmed to rest on a stake.

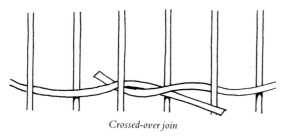

Crossed-over join

Laid-in join: This is neat but requires careful trimming. It is most suitable where the stakes are very close together. The old end is brought to the front and the new end inserted to the right of it.

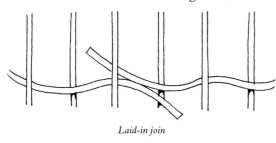

Laid-in join

Pricked-in join: This is neat and fairly strong but it is a little fiddly and takes longer to do. It needs to be done well to be unobtrusive and its advantage is that there are no ends to trim later or to snag on anything. The old end is cut to a point, bent at a right angle and pushed down into the weaving to the left of a stake. The new end is cut, bent and pushed down into the work to the right of the same stake.

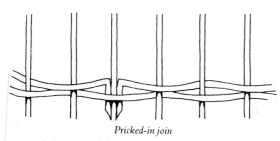

Pricked-in join

Half-pricked-in join: This is fairly strong if trimmed correctly. It cuts down by half the number of ends to be trimmed. The old end is brought to the front and the new end cut, bent and pushed down into the weaving to the left of the old end and to the right of the stake. The new end is then worked by crossing over the old end.

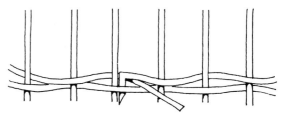

Half-pricked-in join

Laid-together join: This join is used for flat materials such as lapping cane or tape and is neat if the material is not too thick. The weavers are worked together for as long as necessary for the join to hold.

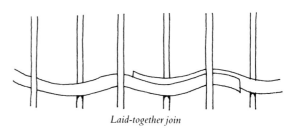

Laid-together join

Follow-on randing

This is the weave you use if you want to rand but have an even number of stakes.

How it is done: Start a weaver off as for randing and in the space immediately behind it start another weaver going over and under the stakes the alternate way. Continue in this manner, making sure you keep the bottom weaver ahead all the time.

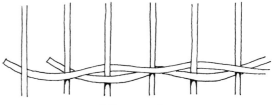

Follow-on randing

English randing

This is a willow weave which allows the tapering nature of the rod to create a very neat weave and which eliminates joining. It can be done on any number of stakes. A diagonal line is created where the butts are put in, but as long as that is taken into account in the design it will not detract in any way.

How it is done: Select as many rods as there are stakes in the basket, choosing ones that are of the same length and thickness. Put a butt end in behind a stake and rand with it all the way to its tip. Put another butt into the next space to the right of the first one and weave that round. Make sure that the tip finishes in the next space along from the last tip. It does not matter if the rods do not go all the way round but if they do, cut them when they get back to the beginning; do not overlap them. Continue in this manner until you have a weaver in every space.

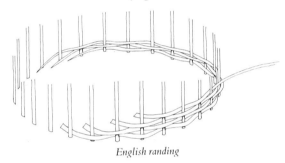

English randing

You then have to decide whether to work another complete set or use a different weave. The disadvantage with this weave is that you must work in complete sets of weavers if you want a level edge.

French randing

This is a very neat and attractive weave, particularly in willow work, but it is also very useful in coloured work because of the diagonal stripes that can be created with it. Its disadvantage is that you have to work with as many weavers as there are

spaces between the stakes, all at the same time (unlike English randing); this takes up a lot of space when working in willow, and in cane the weavers can get very tangled. You also have to beware, when using willow, of the rods drying out, which they will do very fast unless you are working in a cool, damp atmosphere. To prevent this you have to work quickly, which is not always conducive to neatness. French randing can be done on any number of stakes.

How it is done: Select as many evenly sized willow rods as there are stakes. Insert a weaver, butt end, into a space and work it in front of a stake, behind the next stake, and back to the front again. Start a second weaver in the space to the left of the first and do the same. Carry on like this until you have a weaver in every space. When you get back to the beginning, check that this is the case – it is easy to miss one out at this point. At the finish of each round you will find two spaces each containing two weavers; in order to complete the round you need to work the two lower weavers in turn. Start the second row by taking any weaver and working it in front of a stake, behind the next, and back out to the front again. Work each weaver in turn like this.

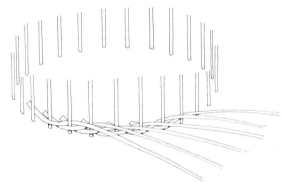

French randing

Below: *Detail of follow-on randing using two different widths of plastic tape*

When you have reached the tips on the first set of weavers you will have to decide whether to add another complete set of rods and, if so, whether to start them with butts or tips. Bear in mind that it is always easier to work from the butt to the tip because of the weight of the rod being at the butt end. It is also easier to control the shape when starting with butts, but if you start butts on top of tips you will end up with a ridge.

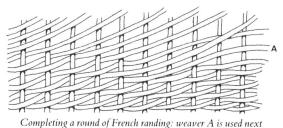

Completing a round of French randing: weaver A is used next

Rib-randing

This is a weave with a pronounced diagonal pattern and can be worked in two ways, depending on the number of stakes you have.

With a number of stakes that does not divide by 3 – how it is done: Insert a weaver into a space and take it in front of two stakes and behind one. Continue in this manner.

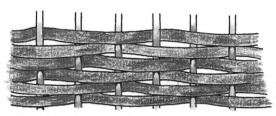

Rib-randing with the diagonal pattern running from bottom left to top right

With a number of stakes that does divide by 3 – how it is done: Use three weavers in three consecutive spaces and chase the weavers as in follow-on randing, but using the over-two-behind-one pattern. Keep the right-hand weaver ahead all the time.

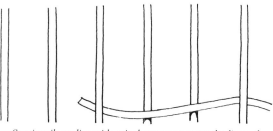

Starting rib-randing with a single weaver to create the diagonal pattern running from bottom left to top right

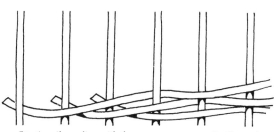

Starting rib-randing with three weavers to create the diagonal pattern running from bottom right to top left

Slewing

This is randing with more than one weaver and is often used on willow bases. Slewing can be done in both cane and willow, and it requires an odd number of stakes. In willow it is an economical weave because short pieces can be used up. You can use any number of rods from two to six but the more rods in the slew the stouter the stakes need to be. In cane it is usually necessary to have bye-stakes (see page 49).

Below: *Detail of rib-randing*

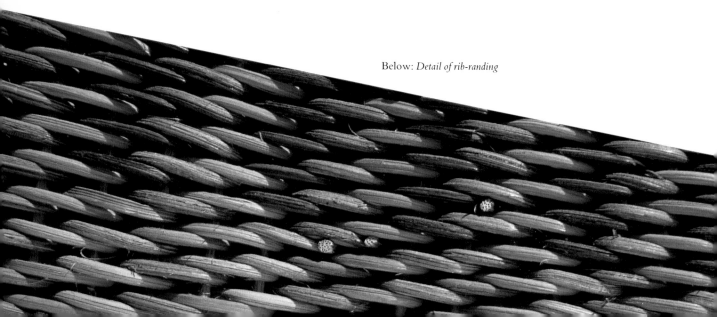

Three-rod slew – how it is done: If using **willow** this weave works best when all the rods are a similar length, so if you have a mixed bundle of tips you would make life easier and your work neater if you sort them first into short, medium and long rods. Use them in that order: all the shorts first, followed by the mediums and then the longs.

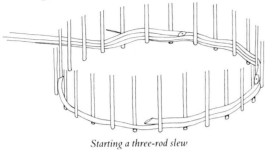

Starting a three-rod slew

Insert the butt end of a weaver into a space and rand one third of its length, then add another weaver, butt end in, on top and work the two together until about one third of the top one has been used. Add another butt and work the three rods together. When the bottom rod runs out, leave the tip on the outside and add another butt at the top. Continue in this manner.

If using **cane** it may be necessary to use bye-stakes to counteract the combined strength of the two weavers used as one. The start is staggered in the same way as with willow. Joins are made when needed, using the laid-in join (see page 24).

Follow-on slewing

This can be used when you want to slew but have an even number of stakes.

How it is done: Start two sets of weavers on opposite sides of the basket – but check that you start the second set in such a way that a weaver will go in front of a stake wherever a weaver from the first set went behind. Chase the two sets. Finish by working the tips out to their ends.

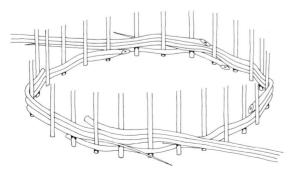

Starting a three-rod follow-on slew

Packing

This is randing used to create hill-shaped blocks. It is a technique that I use a lot, mainly to create colour patterns rather than alter the form of a piece, but it can be used for either purpose. It can be worked in cane or willow.

How it is done: Packing, in order to be unobtrusive, really has to be done with a single weaver because at the end of each row this turns round a stake and is worked back again. With more than one weaver a hole would be created in the weaving where the turn is made. Making the sharp turns required in packing can cause cane and willow weavers to crack, no matter how well prepared the material is. In that case, twist the weaver as you turn it around the stake; this usually cures the problem. You can use packing to make small bumps or big ones:

To make a small bump: Decide how many stakes you want to create the bump over, and start by putting the weaver in to the left of the left-hand stake. Rand across to the stake furthest on the right of your selected block and when you reach it, turn the weaver around the stake. Work back to the left again, but this time turn on the stake before last. Continue like this until you have no stakes left, then leave the end at the back.

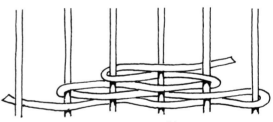

Packing to create a small bump

To make a big bump: Decide how many stakes you want to create the bump over, then start your packing on the central two stakes. Weave back and forth, going one stake further each time until you are weaving across the chosen number of stakes. Then work back in again, going to one less stake each time until you have no stakes left. Leave the end at the back.

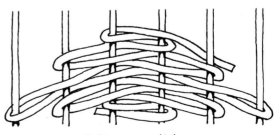

Packing to create a big bump

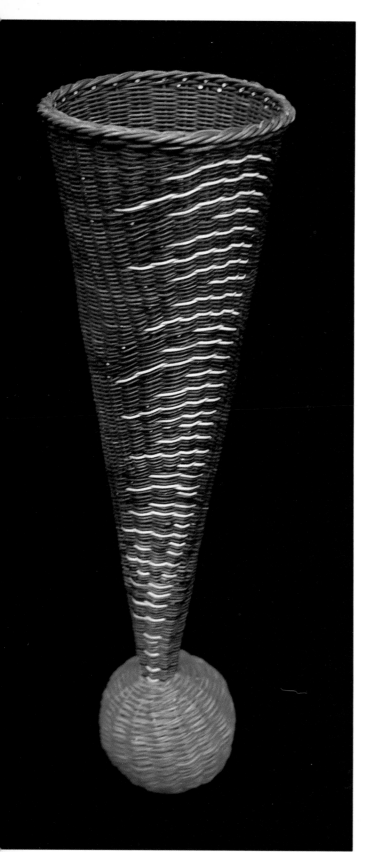

Joins: If you need to join whilst packing, use any of the joins suitable for randing (see page 23).

Filling-in: Often when levelling up the edge of a basket that has a lot of packing in it, I find it necessary just to fill in as required, not necessarily going only one stake more or less each time. This works fine as long as turning twice on the same stake is avoided.

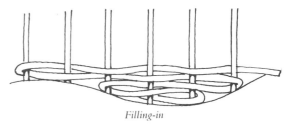

Filling-in

Step and zig-zag patterns: You may want to create a raised area and use the holes that result by turning more than once on the same stake as part of the design. In this case, use the packing technique but turn on the same stake for several rows before increasing or decreasing the number of stakes you weave over.

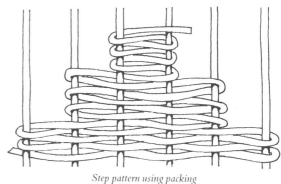

Step pattern using packing

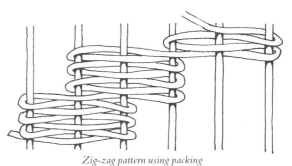

Zig-zag pattern using packing

Left: *Cane umbrella basket showing randing on the cone; height c. 70 cm (27½ in)*

Pairing Weaves

Pairing

This style of weaving is so called because it always involves a pair of weavers. It is a neat and strong weave, usually used at the start of round bases in cane and willow and often for working the entire base. It is used on oval bases, too, but only in combination with reverse pairing or randing in order to avoid the base twisting, which it will do unfailingly and infuriatingly if you use pairing alone. It can be used anywhere else on a basket as well.

Pairing gives the basket maker good control over the stakes, because they are trapped in between two weavers at once. It is therefore a particularly useful weave when you are working on complicated or voluptuous shapes. Any number of stakes can be used.

How it is done: Pairing is started either by laying in two weavers in two consecutive spaces or by looping a single weaver around a stake. The weave is created by taking the left-hand weaver and crossing it over the right-hand weaver, taking it behind the next stake and back to the front. Continue in this manner.

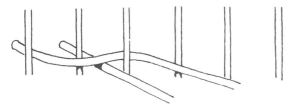

Starting pairing by laying in two weavers

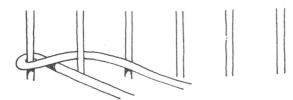

Starting pairing by looping a weaver around a stake

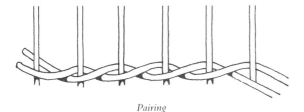

Pairing

Right: *Detail of pairing*

Joins: As with randing, the type of join to use depends on the material being worked, the position of the join in the basket, and the degree of strength required. These are some of the options:

Laid-in join: The weaver to be joined should be in the left-hand position. Pull the end of it towards you and lay the new end immediately to the right of it, under the other weaver which holds the join in place as you make it. The new weaver is then used straight away and the ends are trimmed later. You must take great care when trimming the ends not to cut them too short, thus causing them to spring out. This is a neat join, most suitable when the stakes are close together or when the weavers are fairly bulky. It can be used for cane and willow, but when using willow remember that joins are usually made butt to butt and tip to tip.

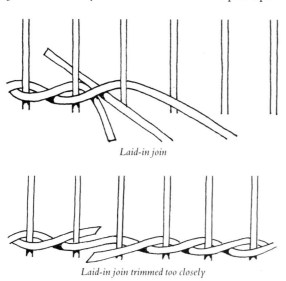

Laid-in join

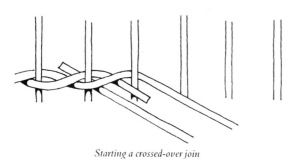

Laid-in join trimmed too closely

Crossed-over join: The weaver to be joined should be in the left-hand position. Push the new end under both weavers to the left of the short end. Take the new weaver and cross it over the old end, then carry on as normal. The ends are trimmed to rest on the stakes. This is a strong and neat join, particularly suitable on bases, but it may be too bulky where stakes are close together or when joining willow butts.

Starting a crossed-over join

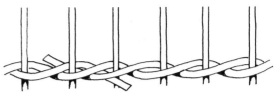

Completed crossed-over join

Interlocked join: The weaver to be joined should be in the left-hand position. Push the new weaver up into the space between the weavers to the left of the short end and behind the stake. Take the new weaver and cross it under the short end, then carry on as normal. This is a slightly more complicated version of the crossed-over join, but it is very strong and particularly suitable where there is a large gap between the stakes. Again, however, it may be too bulky in some circumstances.

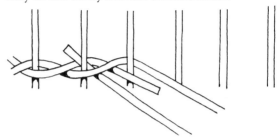

Starting an interlocked join

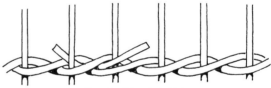

Completed interlocked join

Left-at-back join: This join is probably the least satisfactory for strength. There is the same danger of the ends springing out that you get with the laid-in join, so the trimming has to be done carefully. It does, however, have an aesthetic advantage because both the ends are left at the back of the work. This can be very desirable when working with dyed cane, which displays its white innards when trimmed. The resulting white blobs can be visually distracting on an all-colour piece, unless they form part of the design.

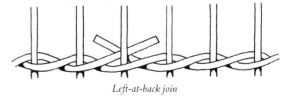

Left-at-back join

Left: *Cane bowl worked with a combination of randing, packing and pairing; diameter c. 50 cm (19¾ in)*

Finishing pairing: As a general rule when working in cane you should try to finish your pairing in the same place as you started so that there is an equal number of rows; otherwise there will be a bump or a dip where you have finished. (The exception is when you are intentionally aiming at an irregular shape.) When working with willow this is not necessary because the work can be rapped level, and by finishing with the tips they will just blend into the top row. Whichever material you use, the ends are then either left at the back or threaded away.

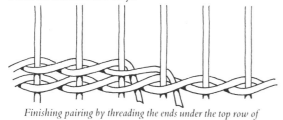

Finishing pairing by threading the ends under the top row of weaving

Reverse pairing

This is the mirror image of pairing and can be used in all the same places. It can be worked in two different ways, although the result is the same: either with the weavers at the front of the work or, on bases, with the weavers at the back of the work. Working with the weavers at the back is quicker because you do not have to work under the other weaver, but it is not suitable for the side of a willow basket as the rods would get kinked in the confined space inside the piece.

French willow baskets often have reversed paired bases and I assume they are done like that for convenience in the workshop. The rods are kept down, away from the worker, instead of flapping about round the neighbouring workers' ears.

Strangely, whenever I see a reverse paired base it strikes me as being neater than a paired one, but after trying several of each to check this, I came to the conclusion that it was just a case of familiarity breeding contempt – there seems to be no logical reason why reverse pairing should be neater.

You can also achieve the same effect as reverse pairing by turning the work over and working pairing right to left instead of left to right; but this rather defeats the object of working with the good side towards you in order to better control its appearance.

How it is done: With the weavers at the front, the left-hand weaver goes *under* the right-hand one, behind the next stake and out to the front. With the weavers at the back, the left-hand weaver comes through between the stakes *over* the right-hand weaver and the next stake, then goes through to the back where it is left.

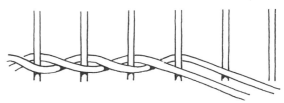

Reverse pairing with weavers at the front of the work

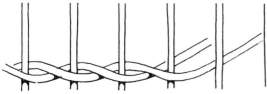

Reverse pairing with weavers at the back of the work

Above: *Cane platter showing pairing with two colours to create the stripes; diameter c. 70 cm (27½ in)*

Joins: All the same methods of joining as for pairing can be used, but the new weavers are pushed in from the back instead of the front; in other words, the whole process is back to front.

Chain pairing

This weave is so called because it looks like the links of a chain. It is done by alternating one row of pairing with one of reverse pairing. It is particularly useful for oval bases (it prevents the base from twisting) and for creating decorative effects. Either one set of weavers can be used or two.

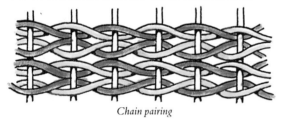

Chain pairing

Using one set – how it is done: This requires that you change from pairing to reverse pairing and vice versa for every row. Whilst it is possible to make the change-over invisible on the outside of the work, it will alter the pattern slightly on the inside. Because all the change-overs come in the same place, it would therefore be unsuitable for a basket where the inside is clearly visible.

Work one round of pairing. When you have come back to the beginning and the right-hand weaver is in the space immediately to the left of the first weaver at the start, work the right-hand weaver again in front of a stake, behind the next, and out to the front again. Then work the left-hand weaver similarly.

Chain pairing with one set of weavers: first move in the change-over from pairing to reverse pairing

Chain pairing: second move in the change-over from pairing to reverse pairing

The weavers are now in position to reverse pair. Complete a circuit, then start the change-over to pairing again when the left-hand weaver is in the space before the start. Weave it over a stake and behind the next stake, then out to the front. The ends are now ready to pair again. Continue in this manner, changing over on each round.

34

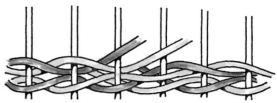

Chain pairing: first move in the change-over from reverse pairing to pairing

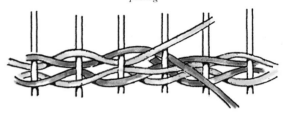

Chain pairing: second move in the change-over from reverse pairing to pairing

Using two sets – how it is done: This is an easier way to achieve the same effect (because you do not have to remember to change over on every row). Start one set of weavers using pairing and half-way around the basket start another set using reverse pairing, then just chase both sets. You can start the two sets next to each other but this does result in an obvious step in the weave at that point.

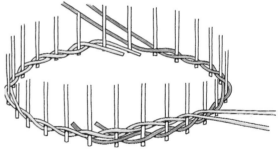

Chain pairing with two sets of weavers

Fitch pairing or fitching

Fitching looks like reverse pairing but it is specifically a row of weaving above a space. If you want to create gaps in the weaving, fitching is the weave that you would use to prevent the weaving above the space slipping down. It can also be used to alter the shape of the basket by spreading the stakes further apart or bringing them closer together. Unlike pairing, fitching can have more than one twist between the stakes; in fact, it should have as many as the space warrants because the object is to trap the stakes very tightly in between the weavers. Fitch pairing is always illustrated as a reverse pair or a chain pair, but I do not think there is a logical reason why it cannot be done using ordinary pairing.

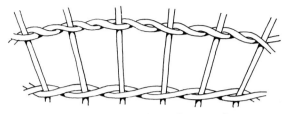

Fitching used to widen the gaps between stakes

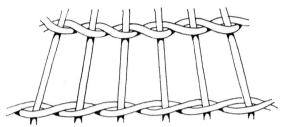

Fitching used to narrow the gaps between stakes

How it is done: If using **cane**, start by looping a weaver around a stake. Try to use a length of cane that will not require joining in the row of fitching.

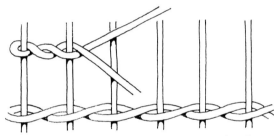

Starting fitching in cane by looping a weaver around a stake

If using **willow** the technique is the same, either by placing two rods tip to tip, overlapping them by 30 cm (12 in) or so, looping the overlapped tips round a stake and then working the two together until the tips run out; or by looping a rod near the butt end and then joining a new butt to the short end in the next space or soon after. Both rods must be of the same thickness in order for the tension to be correct and for the fitching to look good, so join in new rods when the old ones get too thick or thin.

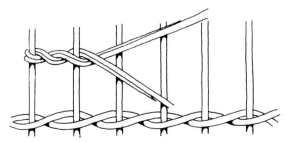

Starting fitching in willow using two rods, tips together

The weave is done in the same manner as reverse pairing with the ends at the front, except that there may be more twists between the stakes. In order to get the twists even it helps to hold both weavers with your right thumb on top of them and twist both together towards you.

Joins: Like joins in pairing the weaver to be joined should always be in the left-hand position. Push the new weaver down into the space just to the left of the short end and behind the stake. Cross it over the short end and carry on as normal. If you are using more than one twist the method is the same. When using willow the joins should be made butt to butt and tip to tip. Sometimes it is necessary to manipulate the finished join a bit to make it look right because the new weaver tends to lie straight rather than at the same angle as the rest of the weaving.

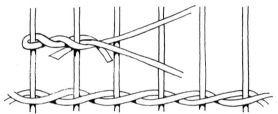

Starting fitching in willow with a butt end and joining a new butt

Finishing fitching: There are two ways of doing this. The first is to thread the two ends into the first loop. The left-hand end goes up into the loop behind the stake and the right-hand end goes down into the loop behind and to the right of the stake. If the fitch is tight this will hold well.

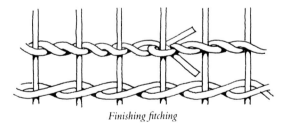

Finishing fitching

(Continued overleaf)

The other way to finish is to continue fitching past the start for several stakes and then tuck the ends into the previous row. This creates a wider portion of weave at the overlap, but it need not detract from the appearance if due consideration has been given to its position in relation to the basket as a whole. The overlap should be rapped down so that the top edge of the fitch is level.

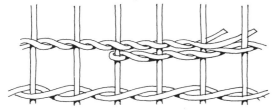

Alternative method of finishing fitching by overlapping the start

Mock pairing

This is a method by which you can turn a row of randing into one that looks as though it has been paired. It is often used when finishing square bases or lids in willow or cane to prevent the randing slipping off the sticks and also to match the row of pairing usually used at the start on a lid. It makes the junction between the randing and the border neater than it would be otherwise. The instructions here are for working from right to left but mock pairing can of course be done from left to right using the same principle.

How it is done: Finish the randing, leaving enough weaver to go back across the sticks once more (in willow, make a join in the previous row if necessary). The next stage depends on whether the weaver is lying in front of or behind the last stick. If the weaver is lying in front of it, take it round behind the stick, through the first space over itself, then in front of the next stick and under the top row through to the back. Continue in this manner. If the weaver is lying behind the end stick, bring it round to the front, under itself through to the back, then to the front again between the next two sticks over itself. Continue in this manner. To finish a row of mock pairing, just cut the weaver to rest against the last stick.

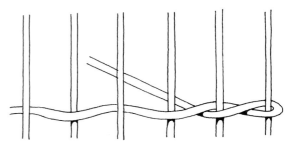

Mock pairing started with the weaver in front of the stake

Stopped pairing

This is pairing that is non-continuous, such as you might find on a lid or other flat panel.

How it is done: Start the pair by looping a weaver around the left-hand stake. Pair as normal until you have a weaver in each of the first and second spaces from the right-hand end. Take the right-hand stake around the last stake and back through to the front. It is then threaded from front to back to lie to the right of the other weaver.

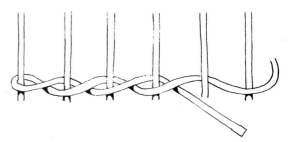

Taking the left-hand weaver around the last stake

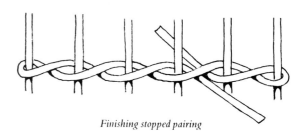

Finishing stopped pairing

Waling Weaves

Waling

This is basically an extended version of pairing. Whereas pairing uses only two weavers (or rods), waling uses three or more. In fact, you can use as many weavers as is practical; most commonly used are wales with three to six rods.

It seems to me that the American use of the term two-, three- and four-strand twining makes the whole matter simpler by eradicating the distinction between pairing and waling. But I like to use the term waling because it is a reminder of the ancient origins of the craft. The word is thought to have come from Old English and Old Norse, in which it had a variety of definitions all to do with creating ridges (in textiles) and holding things in place (in fencing and planking) – both are appropriate to its use in basketry.

Waling is most commonly used at the edge of the base to provide a strong ridge for the basket to sit on, and just prior to bordering where it holds all the stakes in the right place ready for the border. It is also often used to create ledges for lids to rest on and it can be found in every other place on a basket, often used decoratively because of its rope-like appearance.

Waling can be done either in cane or willow, and the principle is the same for any number of weavers: each weaver goes in turn in front of one less stake than the number of weavers being used and then behind one.

Three-rod wale – how it is done: Put three weavers into three consecutive spaces (in willow, start with tips). Take the left-hand weaver in front of two stakes, behind one, and then bring the end out to the front again. Continue in this manner.

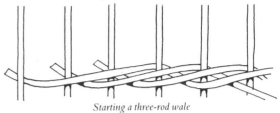

Starting a three-rod wale

Four-, five- and six-rod wales – how they are done: These are worked in exactly the same way, but going over more stakes – three for a four-rod, four for a five-rod, and so on. The more rods you use in a wale the bigger it will be, obviously, but it will also appear looser. So, the wales with more rods tend to look better when the stakes are not too far apart or, as in the case with willow, when the stakes are stout enough to use heavy rods.

Joins: These are done in the same way as a laid-in join in pairing (see page 30) and are made when the rod you want to join is in the left-hand position. In willow, joins are done butt to butt and tip to tip.

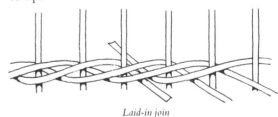

Laid-in join

Below: *Three-rod waling showing the effects created by using different numbers of stakes*

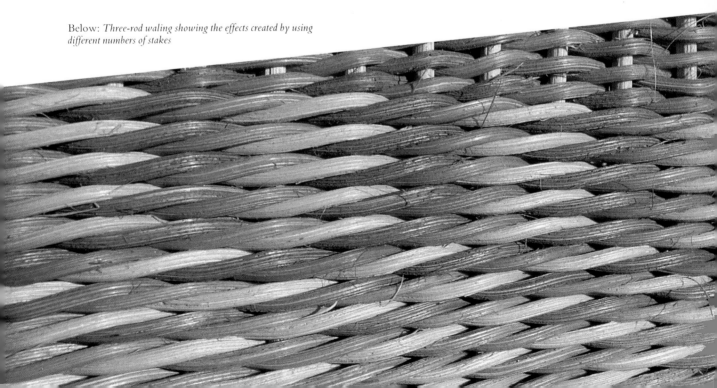

Finishing a single row of three-rod waling: If using **cane** and you are working just one row of waling it is necessary to join the start and finish. When the weaver you have just worked is in the same space as the one at the start, leave it there, lying to the left of the first one. The next weaver then goes over two stakes and behind one as normal, but is then brought out to the front by tucking it under the weaver already there, and to the left of the short end. The last weaver is then taken over two stakes and behind one as normal, and brought to the front by tucking it under the two weavers already there, to lie to the left of the short end.

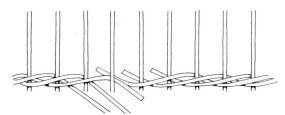

First stage of finishing a row of waling

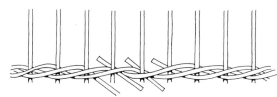

Second stage of finishing a row of waling

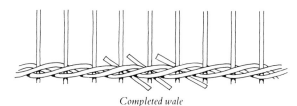

Completed wale

If using **willow** you should aim to start and finish a row of waling with tips (which will mean joining the rods butt to butt at some point on the way round). That way you can overlap the tips at start and finish, which should then equalize the depth of the wale all the way round.

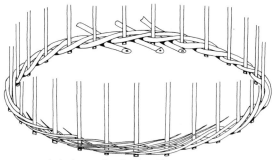

A single row of waling in willow using two sets

If the rods are quite long and heavy you can use the same method as for cane. In this case, start the rods a little way from the tips so that there is not too much difference in the size of the rod at the start and finish.

Working more than one row of waling: Because waling creates such a pronounced ridge it is necessary when using a regular-sized material like cane to complete each round of waling before starting the next if you are working only a few rows. If you continue weaving without finishing each row the wale will spiral up over the start – and the more weavers there are in a wale the more pronounced the spiral will be – and then it will be difficult to finish it so that the weaving looks level.

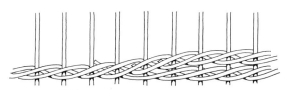

Working a second row of waling: spiralling

This can be overcome by cutting the weavers and finishing each row as already described, then starting the second row of waling with another set of weavers. But there is also a way to do it without cutting the weavers, called 'stepping-up' or 'changing the stroke'. This technique is probably one of the hardest for beginners to grasp, but it is worth learning.

Stepping-up, whilst neat, is really only appropriate if you want to do a few rows of waling. Too much stepping-up in the same place on a basket tends to distort the shape at that point, so if you want to wale the entire piece I should plan to do it without using this technique. Stepping-up is not necessary when using willow because of the irregularity of the material.

Stepping-up a three-rod wale – how it is done: When the weaver you have just used comes out to the front in the space *before* the one in which the first end lies, you have reached the point where you must step-up. Take that same weaver and work it in front of two stakes, behind one, and then bring it out to the front again. Take the next weaver to the left of the one you have just worked and repeat the process. Then do the same with the last weaver.

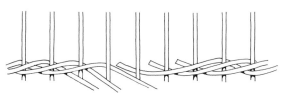

The position of the weavers for starting the step-up

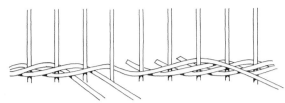

First stage of the step-up

What you have done, in effect, is work the last three movements in reverse order, with the result that the weavers should now be sitting on top of the previous row ready to start a new row in the normal manner. Four-, five- and six-rod step-ups are worked using exactly the same principle.

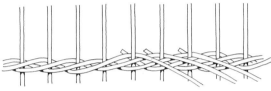

Completed step-up

Dropping a rod – how it is done: When you are upsetting a basket (see page 49) it is often necessary to work a four-rod wale around the edge of the base and then work a couple of rows of three-rod wale to hold the uprights in the right position for the side weaving. It is possible to go from a four-rod to a three-rod wale, a process known as 'dropping a rod', and step-up at the same time.

If using **cane**, work a four-rod wale one stage further than you would for a three-rod step-up, so that the weaver you have just used is lying in the same space as the left-hand short end. Now drop that weaver and cut it to about 5 cm (2 in) so that you know it is finished with. This also marks the spot where you will need to do your step-up on future rows. Step-up with the remaining three rods but take them over three stakes and behind one, even though you no longer have four rods. This is because you are still completing a four-rod wale. Your three weavers will now be in position for you to start a three-rod wale.

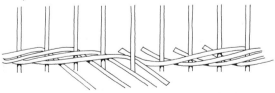

Preparing to change from a four-rod wale to a three-rod wale in cane

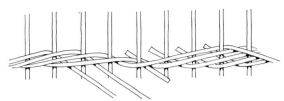

First stage of change from a four-rod wale to a three-rod wale

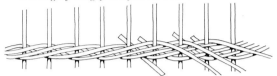

Completed step-up

If using **willow** the technique is slightly different and is usually done by dropping the rod that is in the space before the one where the four-rod wale was started, then carrying on as normal.

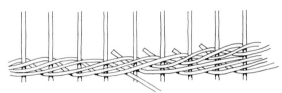

Changing from a four-rod wale to a three-rod wale in willow

Finishing a block of waling which has not been stepped-up: If using **cane**, try to finish in the same place as you started and either lay the ends to the back in order or tuck them under the top row.

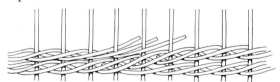

Finishing a block of waling where no stepping-up has been done, leaving the ends at the back

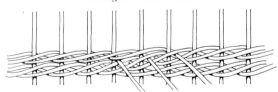

Alternative method of finishing a block of waling where no stepping-up has been done, tucking the ends under

If using **willow**, as with pairing you should try to finish a row of waling with tips so that they will blend into the top row.

Reverse waling

This is the mirror image of waling. Its use is mainly decorative and it can be done with as many rods as is practical.

Three-rod reverse wale – how it is done: Start by putting the ends of each weaver in between two stakes, but instead of leaving the end at the back as in ordinary waling, bring it out to the front again in the next space to the left. Insert the weavers in order from right to left. The left-hand weaver is then worked in front of two stakes underneath the other two weavers, behind the third stake, and out to the front again. Continue in this manner.

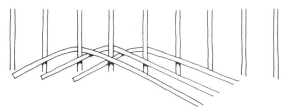

Starting a three-rod reverse wale

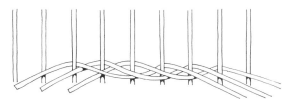

Working a three-rod reverse wale

Joins: Where necessary, use the laid-in join (see page 30) but work it from the back of the piece.

Laid-in join for reverse waling

Finishing a reverse wale: If using **cane**, when you get back to the beginning, tuck in the ends, in order, to the left of the ends sticking out to the front and underneath the wale. If you want to work another row without cutting the weavers, bring them to the top of the wale between stakes.

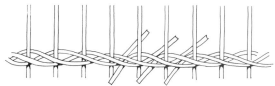

Finishing a single row of reverse waling

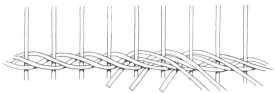

Preparing to continue reverse waling

If using **willow**, follow the same techniques as for cane; or, provided you are finishing with tips, simply continue weaving until they run out.

If you want to work just one round of reverse wale in willow, again follow the same procedure as for cane but do not start the rods right at the tips. Instead, start them where they seem of a reasonable size.

Chain waling

This weave is made up of one row of waling and one row of reverse waling. Used with colours, it can create dynamic patterns.

How it is done: Chain waling can be done by one of three methods. The first involves working a complete row of waling, cutting the ends, and then working a complete row of reverse waling. Alternatively, it can be done by working one row of waling and continuing with the same weavers. Step-up and then take the left-hand weaver over two stakes but under the other two weavers and behind the next stake. When you have completed that row, tuck the ends through to the inside under the wale in the manner already described in 'Finishing a single row of reverse wale in cane'. If you want to continue chain waling, bring the ends back up to the top of the wale between stakes and continue with ordinary waling.

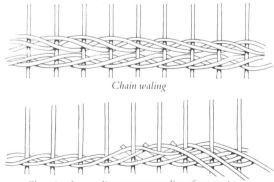

Chain waling

Changing from waling to reverse waling after stepping-up

The third method of chain waling is done by using two sets of weavers as in chain pairing (see page 34).

Left: *Willow and cane shopping basket showing three-rod waling; height c. 48 cm (19 in)*

Padded waling

This is a wale worked over a core to make it larger. It is not a technique that I have ever tried in willow but it is very effective in cane. The number of weavers you use will depend on how far apart the stakes are, how fat the core is, and whether or not you want any of it to show. A fat core and a three-rod wale will leave the core showing, whereas a four-rod wale will probably cover a thinner core. Sometimes it may be necessary to have two weavers in each space in order to cover the core completely.

Padded waling using single weavers

Padded waling using double weavers

Padded three-rod wale – how it is done: For the core, take a piece of cane long enough to go round the basket plus an overlap of 10 cm (4 in) or so. Shave down this amount from one side of one end of the cane to a fine point, then lay the core against the work over the weavers where you want the padded wale to be, leaving the extra 10 cm (4 in) sticking out to your left, with the cut side facing you. Bring the left-hand weaver up over the core and two stakes, take it behind the third stake and out to the front under the core. Continue in this manner with the other weavers.

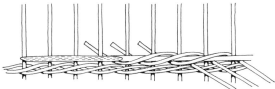

Position of the core when starting padded waling

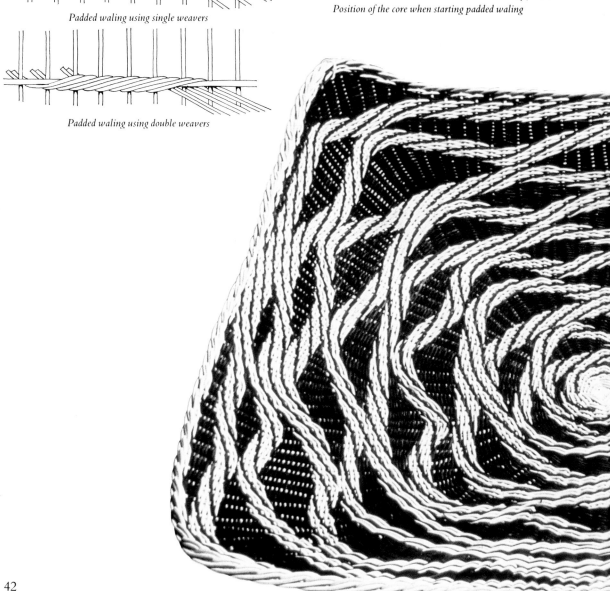

When you get close to the beginning, shave down the inside edge of the cane core so that it exactly matches the other end. In this way when they are laid back together they will be the same width as the rest of the core. Thread the last few weavers over the core so that they hold the two ends together. If the core is still partially uncovered you can work one or more of the weavers around again. The ends of the weavers should eventually finish underneath the core.

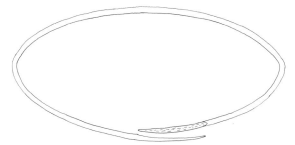

How the core is joined

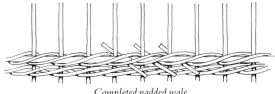

Completed padded wale

Stopped waling

This is non-continuous waling, such as you might find on a lid or other flat panel.

How it is done: Start the waling by inserting a weaver down to the right of the first stake. Take another weaver and loop it around the first stake. Work a three-rod wale as normal, until you have a weaver in each of the last three spaces. Take the central weaver in front of the two stakes to the right, around the last stake, and back through to the front. Then take it over two stakes to the left and thread it under the wale, to lie to the right of the weaver in that space. Trim all the ends.

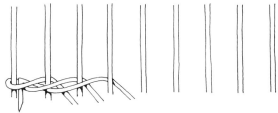

Starting a stopped wale

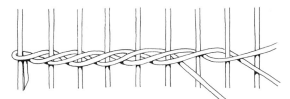

Second stage of a stopped wale

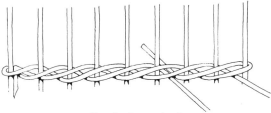

Completed stopped wale

Left: *Cane platter worked with a combination of packing and waling; width c. 50 cm (19¾ in)*

43

Bases

Bases can be made any shape you require and in an infinite variety of ways. The methods I describe here are some of the most common, and are the ones that I use myself. Because I make baskets for a living, I have to be constantly aware of the amount of time involved in the various techniques, and whether or not the end result is worth any extra time. Consequently, I tend to use only those methods that are both quick for me to do and which produce the results I want. If you are making baskets purely for the pleasure of it, however, you need not set yourself any such limitations. Nevertheless, the methods which are included in this chapter will provide you with plenty of scope to be going on with.

Before starting to learn how to make bases, there are a couple of technical terms that you will need to be familiar with:

Rapping: This is tapping or beating the work with a special tool called a rapping iron. Either the flat or the edge of the iron is used. Rapping is done to level off the weaving or to close it up; to knock stakes in at the upsett (see page 49); and to put crams in place (see page 67). It is used mainly in willow work. Randing in willow is known as close randing when the work is rapped down hard.

Slyping: This means making an angled cut on a willow rod. Gripping the knife well, make a cut away from you down towards the butt end of the rod. This can be achieved in one movement with practice and if done correctly will taper the rod to a point. Many willow workers make their slypes by pulling the knife towards the body: this is a safe method provided you are shown properly how to do it. I learnt to make my slypes away from me, however, and find it a very quick, accurate and safe method. It really does not matter which method is used, as long as it produces the desired result without injury.

Slypes are used at the upsett, when cramming-off borders, and to put border stakes, handles and fastenings into the work. They are only necessary in canework when using very heavy canes such as handle cane, because angled cuts can be made simply using side-cutters.

Round Bases

Round bases can be made in any suitable material,
and the principle is the same for willow or cane.

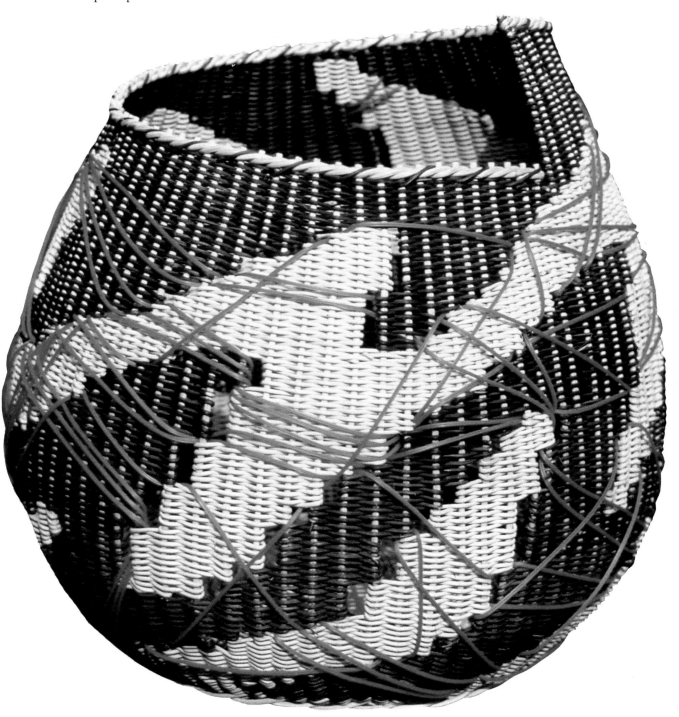

Round-based cane basket; height c. 35 cm (13¾ in)

Size of material

The material used for the base sticks is usually the largest-size material in a basket, and the material for the base weaving is often the finest.

Cane: When using cane you should work on the basis of having weavers which are roughly four or five sizes smaller than the base sticks. You will find that you very quickly develop a sense of what feels right. If the sticks are too thin the weavers will make them bend and if they are too thick the weavers will not control them. As your skill develops, however, you will be able to stretch the range of possibilities.

Willow: With willow you might use the butts of 5 ft (1.5 m) or 6 ft (1.80 m) rods as sticks and 3 ft (1 m) or 4 ft (1.20 m) rods to weave with, but again it is a matter of using the sizes that feel right for the job. On a large basket, for example, you might need sticks from the butts of 8 ft (2.5 m) rods and 5 ft (1.5 m) or 6 ft (1.80 m) rods for weavers.

How many sticks?

The quantity of sticks needed depends on the size of the material, the diameter of the base, and the eventual height and shape of the finished basket. Details of how to work this out for your own designs are given on page 94.

Weaves

Most weaves can be used on a round base. Slewing is very common in willow work and French randing can look especially beautiful on a willow base. If you have an even number of sticks but want to work randing or slewing you can either work the pattern in the follow-on manner, using two sets of weavers, or you can alter the number of sticks by cutting one out or adding one. Do this just before separating the pairs of sticks into singles.

I use pairing a lot for round bases because it is a strong and neat weave, which is the most important thing if the base is not going to be visible when the basket is finished.

A paired base using eight sticks – how it is done: The sticks are cut from prepared material 2.5–4 cm (1–1½ in) longer than the finished diameter of the base. If using **willow**, keep the natural curve of the rods, if there is any, and do not straighten them out.

Pierce four of the sticks in the centre using a medium-sized bodkin and stretch the slot by working the bodkin from side to side. Then thread the other sticks through the slot. This is

46

called the slath. With willow, pierce the sticks with the curve going the same way and alternate butts and tips.

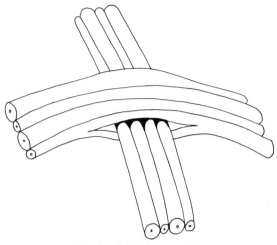

The pierced slath for a round base

Tying in the slath: If using **cane**, take a weaver and loop it around one of the arms of the slath. Pair around twice, treating the four bunches of sticks as though they are single sticks. On the third row, separate the bunches of sticks into twos and pair around for two more rows, then separate them into single sticks. Continue pairing, doming the base very slightly away from you as you work to create an upside-down saucer shape. This helps the finished basket to sit well and also prevents the centre of the base wearing away in use. Make joins using the crossed-over method for strength (see page 30).

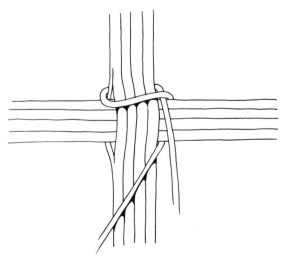

Tying in the slath using cane

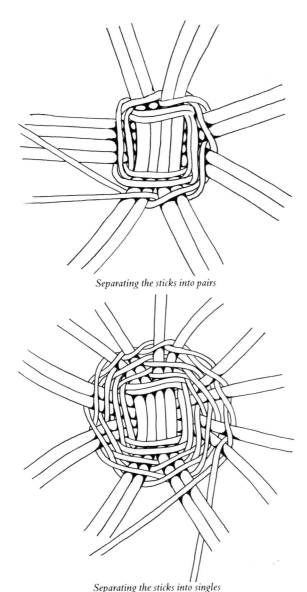

Separating the sticks into pairs

Separating the sticks into singles

When you reach the diameter that you want, weave around until you are level with the point where you started, then thread the ends through from the back (see 'Finishing pairing', page 32). Trim the ends of the sticks flush with the weaving and trim the joins.

Finished base, slightly domed

If using **willow** the slath can be tied in several ways, starting either with butts or tips. The method I use is to take the two finest weavers I can find and push both butts into the slot cut in the sticks. Pair around in exactly the same way as for cane, cutting the two butt ends flush with the slath when you get back to them. Continue weaving, joining tips to tips and butts to butts.

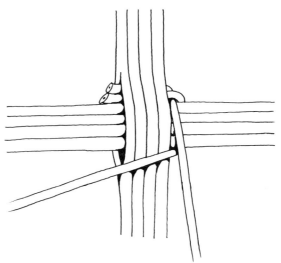

Tying in the slath using willow

I start with butts rather than tips because they are thick enough to make the first four rows of weaving look good. By the time you have reached the point where the sticks are separated into singles the rod is fairly thin, thus making it easy to work into the small spaces.

Carry on weaving the base in the same manner as for cane, doming it as you go. With willow, however, it is not necessary to stop at the same point as you started because the willow tapers and the rows are not therefore of an equal width. Simply stop when the base is a regular shape. It is preferable to finish with tips because they will blend smoothly into the outer edge. Tuck the ends under the top row of weaving (as shown in 'Finishing pairing', page 32) and cut the sticks flush with it. Afterwards, trim any joins. This is called 'picking off'.

Round and oval bases in either willow or cane look horrible and are weakened if they are badly woven, by which I mean having lots of gaps in the weaving where the sticks are opened out. It is not easy to get the weaving close at first but it helps to take the opening out of the sticks one movement at a time, making sure that each weaver is exactly where you want it before working the other one. The opening out of the sticks is made easier if you pull them well apart before trying to weave between them. Provided that the material has been properly prepared the sticks will not break.

Staking-up: If using **cane**, cut your stakes to the desired length from dry cane two to four sizes smaller than the base sticks. (Details of how to determine the length of your stakes are given on page 94.) Each stick on the base requires four stakes, two at each end of it, so for an eight-stick base you will need thirty-two stakes. Do not damp the stakes yet as it is much easier to push them in dry. Using side-cutters, cut a point at one end of each stake and push them into the base, one each side of every stick, as far as they will go. If any prove difficult, use a bodkin to stretch the space a bit first.

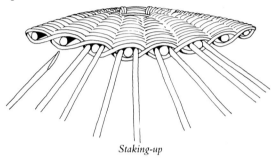

Staking-up

The next stage depends on what shape the finished basket is to have. If you want a gentle bowl shape then just leave the stakes after you have put them in; but if you want the basket to go sharply upwards from the edge of the base, damp the cane and with round-nosed pliers squeeze each stake as close to the edge of the base as possible. Bend all the stakes up and tie tightly together.

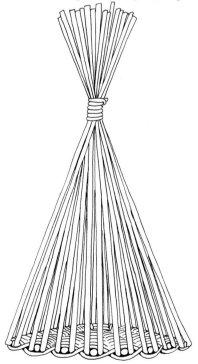

Squeezed stakes tied tightly together

If using **willow** it is not necessary to cut the rods to length: simply choose the length and thickness of willow that is appropriate for your basket, checking that the point on the rod where you will be bending it for the border is of a suitable thickness. The rods should not be too spindly for a basket that is going to be picked up by its rim, such as a wastepaper basket, and not too heavy for the type of border you want.

Choose thirty-two equally sized, mellowed rods, and with a sharp knife make a slype on the butt end of each. Turn your base upside down (concave side facing you) and hold one side of it down on the floor with your foot. Take each rod and with the cut side away from you, push the stakes as far as you can into the base on the side furthest away from you, one either side of each stick. Use both hands on the rod and if it seems difficult either dip the cut end in water or wipe some soap on it.

I put my stakes in cut sides away from me because if they are the other way round, with the cut facing outwards and sticking out beyond the edge of the base, they can crack when you bend them up. This really only applies to small bases where the depth to which the stakes are pushed in is about the same as the length of the slypes. On big bases the slyped part will be pushed well into the base.

Having pushed all the stakes in, turn the whole thing over – you need plenty of space for this – and start the process known as pricking-up. Put the point of a sharp knife half-way through into the rods about 12 mm (½ in) away from the edge of the base and turn the knife in the willow to the right, lifting the rod up at the same time. It will bend at that point. When you have bent all the rods in this way, tie them together tightly at the top and then with a rapping iron knock the point where each rod is bent. This pushes the stakes tight into the base, just that bit further than you are able to do by hand, and the further into the base they are the less likely they are ever to come out again. They also add to the strength of the base. You are now ready to upsett.

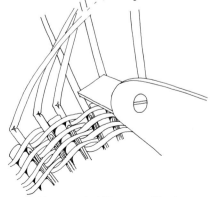

Staking-up and pricking-up a willow base

Upsetting and bye-staking: Upsetting is the process of putting on the rim around the edge of the base that the basket will sit on, and working the first few rows up the sides of the basket that start to determine the shape of it.

If using **cane**, lay the basket on its side with the base towards you. Take four weavers and push them into the left of four consecutive stakes in the same way that you pushed in the stakes. The far left weaver should be on the right of a stick because this helps to trap the dropped rod at the end of the first row. Now work a four-rod wale, making sure that you tuck the weavers down between the stake and stick when you weave around the left-hand stake of a pair. This ensures that you work over the edge and cover the ends of the base sticks. If you do not pull the wale down you will end up working it on the side of the basket rather than forming a ridge at the junction between base and sides.

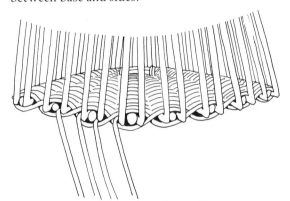

Positioning for weavers at the start of the upsett

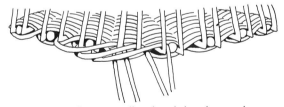

Working the upsett, pulling the rods down between the stakes and sticks

When you reach the beginning again, drop a rod (see page 39), stand the work upright, and continue with a three-rod wale for two more rows. Step-up between the rows. With these two rows you can determine the angle of the sides of your basket by pulling out or pushing in the stakes as you work. You now have the foundation of your basket and all that is required is the side weaving.

At this point you need to decide whether or not your basket requires bye-stakes. Bye-stakes are strengtheners. They enable you to make the sides of a cane basket much stronger without having to use very thick stakes which would make working

the border extremely difficult. They also help you to control the form of the basket because they force you to make a conscious decision to alter the shape. There are few occasions when I would not use bye-stakes – usually a decision to do without them is taken for aesthetic reasons.

Bye-stakes are cut just long enough to go up to the border, where they are trimmed. Cut one bye-stake for every stake and cut a point on one end of each. Insert the bye-stakes into the waling to the right of the stakes, so that their ends are hidden by the stakes when they are bordered down. Bye-stakes can also be cut to the same length as the original stakes if you want to use them either in the border or for making a ledge inside the basket.

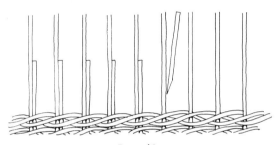

Bye-staking

If using **willow** upsetting can be done either with one or two sets of three or four rods and by starting either with butts or tips:

a) *One set of four rods started with tips:* Lay the basket on its side with the base towards you. Take four rods of equal length and slightly thinner than the stakes and put the tips into the base to the left of four consecutive stakes (in the same manner as for cane). Work a four-rod wale, pulling the weavers well down into the spaces between the ends of the sticks and the stakes. When you get back to the beginning, drop a rod and continue with a three-rod wale for another two rounds. Make joins butt to butt and tip to tip, finishing the waling on tips.

b) *Two sets of rods started with tips:* This method is particularly useful on very big bases where the waling rods are not long enough to go all the way round without joining as it ensures that there are no joins in the upsett which could weaken it. Start one set of rods on each side of the base and chase them.

c) *Two sets of rods started with butts:* This is harder to do than the previous method but it is the one I usually use because I like the appearance of the solid rim around the edge of the base. Lay the basket on its side with the base towards you. Cut slypes on the butts of eight rods and push them into four consecutive spaces and to the left of four stakes on opposite sides of the base. Bend the rods

49

sharply down and if necessary rap them to ensure that they are bent as close to the edge of the weaving as possible. Work a four-rod wale, pulling the rods well down into the spaces between the stakes and the ends of the sticks, and trying not to kink the rods as they go across the stick ends and stakes as this would spoil the appearance. When you reach the start of the other set, either finish the ends off by drawing them through (see page 38) or drop a rod and continue with a three-rod wale.

You are now ready to do the side weaving. Bye-staking is generally unnecessary in willow because you can use a sufficiently strong stake that will be thin enough for the border by the time you get there (because it tapers); but occasionally in fitched work bye-stakes are used. In this case they are usually put into the waling butt end upwards to equalize the width of the two stakes together.

Variations on round bases

It is not always necessary to work a round cane base separately and then stake-up; you can start with a slath of much longer sticks, which can subsequently be used for the sides as well if they are bent upwards, either sharply by working a trac (see page 63) or squeezing the canes, or gently by tightening the weave. The initial slath sticks can be bound or held together differently, too – in as many ways as your imagination can come up with.

Look at any collection of imported basketware in a shop and you will come across other variations. Experiment with these on your own baskets, or better still, invent your own.

Oval Bases

There are two oval shapes in which bases are made: the oblong oval, which has round ends and straight sides, and the elliptical oval, which is more like the shape of an egg. Oval bases can be made in any suitable material and the technique is very similar to that used for round bases. The method I use for oval willow bases is more commonly thought of as a French technique.

In oblong oval bases long and short sticks are used, the long ones running the length of the base and the short ones, spaced at regular intervals, running across the long sticks.

Right: *Oval-based cane shopping basket; height c. 45 cm (17¾ in)*

Size and quantity of material

The same guidelines apply as for a round base.

Weaves

You are slightly more restricted in the type of weave you can work in making an oblong oval base, because the twisted weaves (pairing and waling) cause the whole base to twist. Do not be fooled into thinking that by damping the work and putting it under heavy weights the twist can be permanently cured; it cannot. Instead, it is necessary to counteract the twist formed, either by matching pairing or waling with an equal number of rows of reverse pairing or reverse waling; or by working the entire base in randing; or by combining pairing around the ends with follow-on randing along the sides. It is the pairing along the sides of the oval base that causes the problem and the longer and narrower the base the more pronounced it becomes.

The same applies once you start doing the siding on an oblong oval basket. Too much pairing or waling without reversing it will cause the whole basket to twist, so it is generally safer to use a randed weave. The innovative American basket maker Luther Weston Turner, writing in 1905, suggested that if you reverse paired the entire base, allowing it to twist, and then paired or waled the body of the basket, it straightened itself out; but I would hate to get that far and then discover that it doesn't work!

I usually pair around the ends and follow-on rand along the sides, or use blocks of pairing and reverse pairing, or work the entire base in chain pairing. These weaves all work equally well in willow or cane and look neat. I would not choose to rand an oblong oval base because I find it difficult to separate the stakes neatly. Like a round base, oval bases should be slightly domed.

Even if you get as far as the border of an oval basket without any twisting you may find that the border itself will make it twist. In this case, I find trac or plait borders are the best (see pages 63 and 72); rod borders tend to have a slight twist built into them and therefore exacerbate the problem.

A paired and randed oblong oval base – how it is done: You can use any number of sticks for an oval base, but here I suggest you use four long sticks and nine short sticks, which is an average quantity, suitable for many sizes of base depending on the thickness of material being used. Cut the short sticks 2.5–4 cm (1–1½ in) longer than the required finished measurements. Pierce them and thread the long sticks through (in willow, alternate butts and tips). Put two short sticks together at each end, positioned at a distance from the ends of the long sticks equal to half the short stick length, and spread out the remaining five sticks in between the pairs.

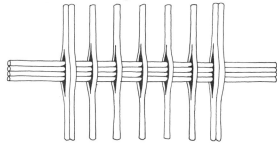

The oblong oval slath

Tying in the slath: If using **cane** the slath can be bound using a length of split chair or round cane. This is mainly a decorative device since it is not essential to hold the slath together. If you decide to use split chair or lapping cane, take a long piece and on the reverse of the slath tuck the end under the first two short sticks. Work a cross on the top side of the slath over the end sticks and then bind the long sticks closely in between the short sticks, crossing each short stick at the back. Use a regular number of binds between each stick. Work a cross at the other end to match the first one and tuck the end away.

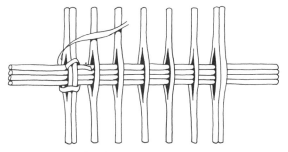

Binding the slath using split chair cane

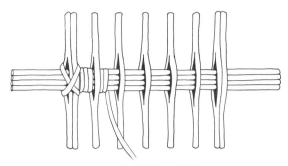

Top side of the bound slath

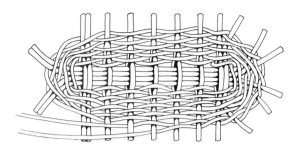

Separating the sticks into singles

If you use round cane, tuck the end into the splits on the first short pair, then continue as for split cane.

The sticks are now held in place and the weaving is started by looping a weaver around the first pair of sticks on the right-hand end of the slath. Pair over these, then over the four long sticks, and over the other pair of short sticks without separating them. Follow-on rand across the single sticks, pairing again when you reach the other end. Continue in this manner. On the third row, separate the four long sticks into pairs and on the fifth row, separate all the pairs of sticks into singles. Continue weaving until you have reached the desired size. If the weaving is a bit loose you may find the sides reach their finished width before the base is long enough. In this case just rap along the sides of the base to close up the weaving, a process which will tend to push the ends out slightly at the same time. Finish the weaving at the point where you started it.

If using **willow** you can also choose to bind the slath with skeined willow instead of cane. The weaving is done in the same manner as for cane, but it is started by putting the butts of two thin rods into the splits – one in the pair of short sticks at the right-hand end of the slath and the other into the single short stick to its left. The weaving can then be continued, using one pair of weavers and joining butts to butts and tips to tips. However, the work will look more regular if you start with two sets of weavers on opposite sides of the slath and chase them.

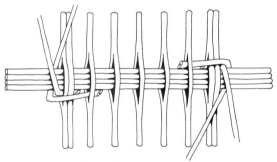

Starting the weaving in willow

Staking-up: This is done in exactly the same way as for a round base except that the single sticks usually get only one stake at each of their ends; all the others get two stakes either side of each end, as before. The technique is the same whether you are working in cane or willow.

The positioning of the stakes along the sides depends on whether or not the basket is to have a cross handle from one side to the other. If it is you need to ensure that the spaces where the handle liners will go are opposite each other in the centres

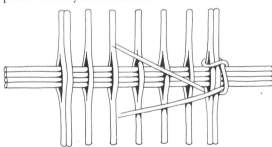

Starting the weaving (note: slath has not been bound)

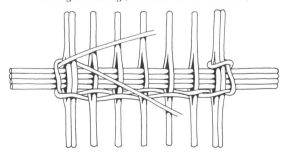

Weaving the base using pairing at each end and follow-on randing along the sides

of the sides. Handle liners are usually put in to the left of a stake. If you have an odd number of short sticks (so that there is one central stick), stake-up to the right of the short sticks. If you have an even number of short sticks (and therefore two central sticks), stake-up to the left of them.

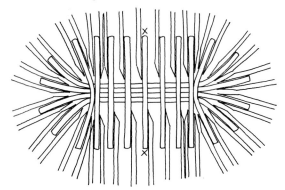

Staking-up with an odd number of short sticks: X marks the position of the handle bow

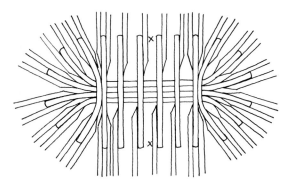

Staking-up with an even number of short sticks: X marks the position of the handle bow

Alternatively, if you have an odd number, use one stake either side of the central stick, then work the two stakes as one, thus creating a channel between the stakes for a handle bow to run in.

A cross handle from end to end of the basket does not need to be considered at the staking-up stage because the sticks at the ends are all double-staked anyway.

Upsetting: If using **cane**, work four weavers in exactly the same way as for a round base, starting them at one end of the base. Work one row of four-rod wale then drop a weaver and continue with a three-rod wale for as many rows as required.

If using **willow** upsetting is done in exactly the same manner as for a round base, using any of the already described options.

Elliptical oval

The method used to create an elliptical oval base is, in essence, exactly the same as the technique for round bases, except for the slath.

Tying in the slath: Take eight sticks, two of which have been cut 25 per cent longer than the others. Pierce the six shorter sticks and thread the other two through. Pair around twice. Separate the pierced sticks into singles as quickly as is feasible, probably on the third or fourth row, and then separate the two longer sticks. Continue as for a round base. This method does not cause twisting so any weave can be used.

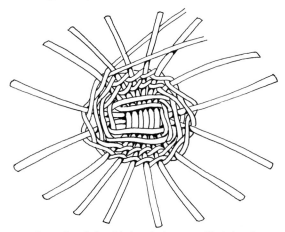

Separating all the sticks into singles on an elliptical oval

Variations on oval bases

The method I use for oval bases is usually referred to as the French or Continental method. What is considered to be the English method does not involve piercing any sticks and uses some rods which double up as both sticks and weavers. I do not use the English method for willow because I find it hard to do well. Thomas Okey refers rather patronizingly in *The Art of Basketmaking* (1932; reprinted 1987 by Dryad Press) to the method I use as being an adapted method suitable for women workers. I don't suppose the many European males who make baskets this way would have been flattered! He does, however, give a good description of how to work the English method.

Right: *Square-based willow and card linen basket; height c. 75 cm (29½ in)*

Square and Rectangular Bases

Like round and oval bases these can be made in any suitable material and the principle is basically the same, although you will need an additional piece of equipment known as a screwblock (see page 19).

Size of material

As always this depends on the size and eventual function of the basket. In general, the sticks on a square or rectangular base of a basket that will get a lot of use need to be stouter than those used on a round or oval base of the same area, so that the base remains flat and rigid. Whether using cane or willow that probably means using sticks double the thickness of the weavers. Otherwise, the same considerations as for round or oval bases apply.

How many sticks?

Again, this will vary from basket to basket. Details of how to work out how many you need are given on page 94.

Weaves

Randing or slewing are most commonly used on square bases. Because weaves are not worked in a circular direction but forwards and backwards on square and rectangular bases, most of the other weaves are unsuitable.

Randed base – how it is done: If using **cane**, start by marking on your screwblock with a pencil or tape the desired width of the finished base. In rectangular work that is the narrowest measurement. Then cut sticks out of cane strong enough for the job in hand and long enough to be pushed into the screwblock plus 2–3 cm (¾–1¼ in). If you want the work to be very flat and rigid, use pairs of sticks; otherwise, use singles in the centre and a pair of sticks, or one thicker stick, at each end. If you use single thicker sticks, shave down one end of each so that the part that goes into the block is no fatter than the other sticks.

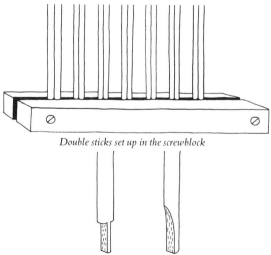

Double sticks set up in the screwblock

Alternative ways of shaving down single thicker sticks

The distance between each stick is determined by how far apart you need your stakes to be at the upsett of the basket. So if you want the base to be 25 cm (9¾ in) wide and your stakes to be 2 cm (¾ in) apart, you will need thirteen sticks spaced 2 cm (¾ in) from centre to centre, plus two extra ones at each end if you are going to double-up the outside sticks. Mark off the 2 cm (¾ in) intervals on the block if it helps. Set the sticks up in the block and tighten the bolts to hold them in place.

Start the weaving by taking a length of cane and making a loop around the left-hand pair of sticks so that one end is just long enough to cross the sticks, plus 4 cm (1½ in). If you have an odd number of sticks, have the short end of the weave to the right when you start; if you have an even number, have the short end to the left.

Pair across the sticks and when you reach the last pair of sticks, take the short end round the outside and tuck it under the other weavers as for an interlocked join (see page 31). Leave the end. Pick up the remaining weaver and continue by randing back and forth across the sticks. If it is important that the edge sticks are completely covered – as, say, for a lid – then it will be necessary to make an extra turn round the outside sticks every so many rows, depending on the thickness of the cane. This is because for every two rows of randing you go round the end sticks only once.

Tucking the short end under the long end to finish it off

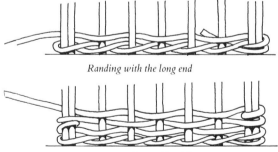

Randing with the long end

Wrapping the outside sticks

Keep a constant check on the width of the base as it is very easy for the edge sticks to start creeping inwards. Remember that this is the foundation of your basket and if this is a regular shape the basket itself is more likely to be as well.

When necessary, any of the joins suitable for randing can be used, but consider whether or not you want all the ends on one side.

When you have reached the desired length of base, work one row of mock pairing to help hold the last row of randing in place and to match the row of pairing that you put on at the beginning. Trim the ends of all but the outside sticks flush with the weaving; by leaving the end ones until later it is less likely that the weaving will fall off whilst you are staking-up.

If using **willow**, set up the sticks in the block in the same manner as for cane, straightening them if necessary as you do it and alternating butts and tips. Work a row of pairing, as for cane, and then continue with randing. It is not normal practice to make any wraps around the outside sticks in willow because you can rap the weaving close if you want to cover the sticks. When you have reached the top, work a row of mock pairing.

On a randed willow base it is quite common for all the rods to be started with butts. This makes the work quicker because you are always working with the heavier end of the rod and consequently it does not flop about as you use it. But you can make the joins butt to butt and tip to tip if you want. Usually joins are just left on one side or the other depending on how the basket is to be used, but any of the randing joins are suitable.

In square work (i.e., bases with right-angled corners) there are two types of corner: a blunt one and a true one. A blunt corner does not actually have a corner stake, so the corner is formed by the stakes on either side of it. A true corner, however, has an added corner post which is usually considerably thicker than the rest of the stakes and is not worked into the border.

Staking-up and upsetting for a blunt corner in cane: Staking-up is done at the ends of the base, in the same manner as for a round or oval base, by pushing the stakes down beside the sticks; the difference is that you usually have only one stake to each stick. If you decide that you want your stakes closer together than you had originally planned you can put two stakes in to each stick or two to every other stick.

Cut your stakes allowing an extra 7–10 cm (2¾–4 in) on the finished height for pushing into the base, plus the allowance for the border. Work out the quantity of stakes needed for the sides by dividing the length of the sides by the distance between each stake, which you have already determined. Cut a point at one end of each stake. Put the stakes into the ends of the base first, to the left of the sticks except for the left-hand edge, where the stake will have to go to the right of the edge sticks. If you have used pairs of sticks on the base you can insert the stakes in the centre of each pair, which will clamp them well in place.

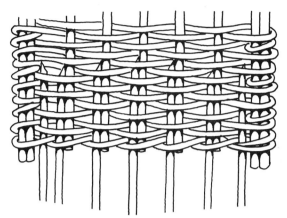

Positioning the stakes when using single sticks

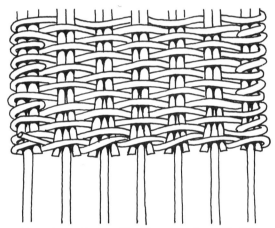

Alternative positioning of the stakes when using double sticks

The side stakes are put in differently. Mark their positions along the sides of the base, putting one stake at each end, 6 mm (¼ in) away from the corner. Using a medium-sized bodkin, put these corner stakes in by piercing through the two outside sticks and the end stake, angling the bodkin upwards as you do so. Push the stake into the hole so that it rests on the second stick. As you pierce the holes along the side you will find they tend to close up again very quickly, so to help the stakes slide in more easily, rub the bodkin on soap or tallow before piercing. When the stakes have been inserted all the way round, trim the ends flush with the base weaving, squeeze the stakes, and tie them up into two bunches, one at each end so as not to distort the base too much. Cut the corner sticks close.

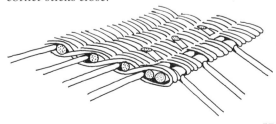

Right: *Staking-up the sides of a square base*

The upsett is started with four canes inserted individually to the left of four sticks at an end, in the same manner as for a round or oval base. Work one round of four-rod wale, keeping the work tight. If your stakes are quite a long way apart you will find that as you go round the corner the canes will tend to sag and not cover it properly. I circumvent this by making a 'false move' on the corner. To do this, leave the weaver that should go behind the first stake around the corner in the corner space so that there are two weavers there. Then carry on as normal. Do this on subsequent rows until it is no longer necessary.

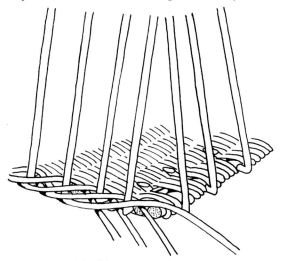

The 'false move' on a blunt corner

When you get back to the start of the upsett, drop a rod, step-up, and continue with a three-rod wale with step-ups for one or two more rows. Concentrate on keeping the weaving tight to the stakes, but do not let the corners creep inwards.

The next stage is to put in the bye-stakes. It can be helpful to bye-stake the corner stakes with slightly thicker cane to help control the shape; in this case they should be put in on the corner side of the stake. You are now ready to continue with whatever weave you like. Keep checking the shape as you work and try to keep the corner stakes as close together and as upright as possible.

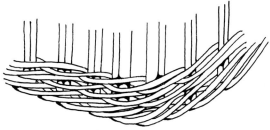

Bye-staking a blunt-cornered basket

Staking-up and upsetting for a true corner in cane: Stake-up in exactly the same manner as for a blunt corner. Cut the corner base sticks very close, then cut four strong corner posts a bit longer than the depth of the sides of the basket. Cut a scoop out of the bottom of each post, so that some of it sticks out below the base initially. This can either be trimmed flush as soon as the corner post is held securely by the weaving, or left to act as feet for the basket.

As you reach the corner with the first row of upsett, place the post cut side against the corner and continue upsetting, treating it as another stake. The second and third rows of waling will hold it in place. When weaving up the sides of the basket, keep the two stakes either side of the corner post as close to it as possible and slightly set in, so that the corner is truly square.

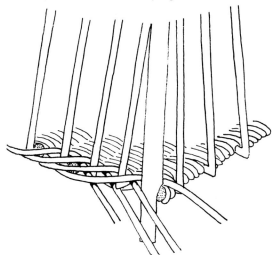

Placing the corner post against the base

There are many ways to stake-up a square basket in willow, but here I deal only with one basic method and one variation that uses the technique known as scalloming.

Staking-up and upsetting for a blunt corner in willow: This is done in exactly the same manner as described for cane, except that the stakes are pricked-up rather than squeezed, and the upsett can be worked in at least two ways:

a) *Using one set of four rods:* Insert four tips into the base at one end to the left of four sticks and work a four-rod wale, keeping the work tight and as close to the base as possible. If the stakes are quite widely spaced it may be necessary to make a 'false move' on the corner (as described earlier) to keep it tight. Drop a rod on the second row and continue with a three-rod wale. Join butts when necessary, finish on tips, and rap the work level.

b) *Using two sets of four rods:* If you want to work one very solid row around the base, insert two sets of four long rods at each end by their butts. Work the upsett in the normal manner, finishing the rods by drawing them through when they reach the start of the other set (as in 'Finishing a single row of three-rod waling', page 38). In order for this to work well the rods should not be too much thinner at the finish of the round than they were at the start. Continue with a single set of three rods, starting them by their tips and working a three-rod wale.

Square base with blunt corners and scallomed side stakes: For this method the stakes are inserted into the ends of the base in the standard manner, but they are scallomed on to the sides of the base.

Cutting a scallom will take some practice. What you are aiming to make is a long, flat, thin and flexible tongue at the butt end of a rod, preferably of an even thickness and approximately 15–25 cm (6–9¾ in) long (depending on the thickness of the willow and the intended distance between the stakes). This means cutting away at least half the thickness of the rod.

Once you have cut your scallomed stakes, push them, cut side up, through the base from underneath, between the outside sticks and the next ones in, until there is only a tiny bit of the cut surface visible on the outside of the base. Then, taking the stake furthest on the right, hold the scallomed end so that it will not slip and lift up the rest of the rod into a vertical position. Lift the scallomed end up to the right of the stake, take it over the stake to the left and lay it down to rest on the base.

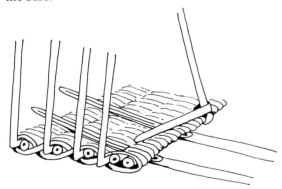

Inserting and knotting on the scalloms

Do the same with the next and subsequent stakes, each time trapping the cut end of the previous stakes. The last end on each side is laid behind the stakes that were inserted at each end. Tying the scalloms on can also be done by working left to right – use whichever method suits you best.

Because this process creates a height differential between the stakes put in at the ends and those scallomed on to the sides (the scallomed ones being higher), various methods of working the upsett have been developed by basket makers to allow for this. The method I describe here is probably the simplest. Using two sets of four rods, insert each set by the tips at the left-hand end of the scallomed sides. The rods should be long enough to reach beyond the start of the other set and preferably almost to the end of that side of the base. Work a four-rod wale as normal, making a 'false move' on the corners if necessary and tucking the rods down well as you work across the ends. Join butts to butts and work another set of either three or four rods, finishing on tips.

This method uses the natural taper of the rods to counteract the difference in height and at the completion of the waling the top edge of the work should be almost level.

True corners in willow: If the basket is to be fairly small the corner post can be fixed in the same manner as for cane. If, however, it is to have a very stout corner post – as for, say, a hamper – it would be better to put in a nail from the underside of the base through the outside sticks and the last row of weaving and then push your corner post onto it after working the first round of upsett. Continue waling, treating the corner post as another stake.

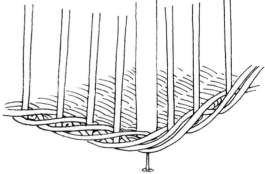

Fixing a corner post in place

Weaving and Shaping the Body

Having staked-up your basket and put in bye-stakes if necessary, you can now settle in one position to weave the body of the basket, in any way you like provided you have enough stakes of the right size.

Traditionally, willow basket makers sit on the floor to work, on a piece of wood known as a plank or on a low box with their legs outstretched. Another plank of wood, known as a lapboard, rests on their thighs and on this the basket stands. It is held down on the board either with a bodkin pierced through the centre of it or with a weight inside. The work is thus held firmly, but at the same time is free to turn. The worker sees the basket side-on and is able to control the shape well this way.

Personally, however, I have never taken to working like that, and many of the shapes that I use would be very difficult to make sitting in that position, being either too big or too shallow. I have a turntable that can be raised or lowered, on which I stand the work with a weight inside, and I sit at it on a normal upright chair. The weight is essential because it holds the work firmly and frees your hands to control the weaving. When I am working on large, flat, cane platters, I often pin them to a wall with a bodkin so that I do not break my back trying to reach across them all the time; but most shapes can be worked quite satisfactorily with the work weighted down on a table.

At this stage of the process you must make a positive decision about the shape of your basket because, given the opportunity, most material would prefer to do something other than what you have planned for it! You have to exercise your will over it with every single movement. As a beginner it seems such a sacrifice to have to undo any work, but if you want to produce a beautiful basket it is essential that you are prepared to undo it occasionally and sometimes even abandon it altogether if the shape is not what it should be.

It is no good just looking at the work every five minutes to check whether it is coming on satisfactorily. Look at the angle of the stakes above the weaving because this is your guide to the finished shape if you continue to work in this way. The shape is determined by how you hold the stakes as you weave over them and how tightly you pull on

the weavers. For example, pushing the stakes in and pulling the weavers more tightly makes the work curve inwards; holding the stakes out and working the weavers loosely brings it out.

Some weaves are better at controlling shape than others. Pairing is easier than randing, and double randing is very hard to control in cane. Slewing in willow is difficult, too, unless the stakes are strong enough. Keep the weavers damp all the time you are working with them; as they dry out, so you will lose control over them.

If the spaces between the stakes become wider than you had originally planned and the pattern and the shape become distorted, add more stakes. Should one of the stakes break and you are not able to replace the whole stake easily, put another one in beside the broken stake, preferably hiding the ends of both pieces behind the weaving.

If you want to make a set of identically shaped baskets it is possible to do so by using a mould. Tie the base onto it after the upsett and work around it. The mould can be a bowl, a tin, or a piece of wood, but make sure that you will be able to take it out of the basket when you have woven around it – in other words, the top of the mould should not be narrower than the bottom.

With the use of packing and by adding and subtracting stakes you should be able to make any shape that you want.

Above: *Cane linen basket; height c. 75 cm (29½ in)*

Borders

Borders can be simple or complicated and as narrow or wide as you like. They are not only found on the top edge or rim of a basket: they are also used to form a 'foot' under the basket in order to raise the base off the ground; to make ledges for lids to rest on; or to create edging for lids. Sometimes wide borders even form the sides of a basket. Most borders can be worked in both cane and willow, though some require considerable skill to do well in willow.

It is usually a good idea to weave at least one row of waling prior to working a border. The wale does three things: first, it gets the stakes into the right position and holds them there; second, it provides a wide, flat surface onto which to work the border; and third, it acts as a visual link between the body of the basket and the border.

After working the wale, cut off any bye-stakes that are not going to be used in the border. Damp or soak the stakes if necessary, then check that the weaving is the same height all the way round. To do this, stand the basket on a flat surface and, using a rigid measure, check the vertical height from the ground to the top edge. Do not measure the actual sides of the basket, unless it is a regular cylindrical shape, because the work may bulge more on one side than another. Remedy any unevenness of height by either rapping the high spots down or gently easing up a low spot with a bodkin. When you are satisfied that the top edge is level, weight the basket down so that it will not jump about while you are wrestling with the border.

Borders are usually worked from the outside of a basket, but occasionally, in cane, you may choose to work from the inside, perhaps in order to leave the ends on the inner side of the basket. In willow, however, it would be very difficult to work a border from the inside because the rods would get bent in the confined space within the basket.

There are basically four types of woven border: trac borders; rod borders; rope borders; and plait borders. Within each type there are infinite variations; this chapter features just some of the ones that I use.

Trac Borders

Trac borders in their simplest form are not very strong and I would not advise using these on a basket that is going to be picked up by its border.

Single-stake trac

This is probably the most straightforward border. Each stake in turn is woven in and out of the others as far as is required before the next one is worked.

How it is done: This can be done in many ways, depending on how many stakes you weave in and out of, and in what pattern. The simplest method is to take each stake, bend it to the right in front of

one or more stakes, and then leave the end at the back, resting against a stake. Continue like this all the way round the basket and when you get back to the beginning, thread the last stake into the loop made by the first.

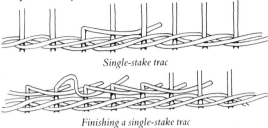

Single-stake trac

Finishing a single-stake trac

Below: *Cane bowl with trac border and two follow-on tracs; diameter c. 47 cm (18½ in)*

Another variation is to start by taking each stake behind one or more stakes, in front of one or more, and then leaving the end at the back. Remember that the more stakes you involve, the more space you will need to leave at the start of the trac into which to thread the last stakes when you get back to the beginning.

Working a behind-one-in-front-of-two trac

If you used a bye-stake in your basket it can be worked with the original stake, treating the pair as a single stake. Alternatively, extra stakes can be added to the right of the original ones and each pair or group of stakes worked as a single one.

If using **cane**, before starting on the border it is a good idea to squeeze all the canes with round-nosed pliers at the point where they will be bent, to make sure the border will be level. To determine at what height that will be, multiply the number of stakes to be woven in and out of by the thickness of the cane. So, for example, if you are going to work a trac that weaves in and out of six stakes and the cane is 3 mm (⅛ in) thick, you need to squeeze the cane 18 mm (¾ in) from the top edge of the weaving. Rather than measuring each stake, which takes time, cut a piece of card the right width and use it as a gauge, placing it on the weaving and resting the round-nosed pliers on it.

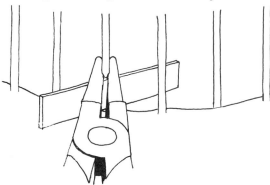

Using a piece of card to measure the correct height at which to squeeze cane stakes

It is not essential to squeeze the canes, in which case a more rounded and springy edge will be created, but this is slightly more prone to unravel if it is a very simple trac.

Single-stake trac worked without squeezing the stakes

If using **willow** you will also need to kink the rods at the right point, but it is not necessary to do them all before starting – only as many as are involved in the pattern you have chosen. From

64

then on you can kink the rod just prior to using it as the height will have been established by the previous rods.

Determine the height at which to kink the first few rods in the same way as for cane. Make the kinks either with a fingernail, a bodkin point, or a knife, depending on how stout the material is.

Trac borders can also be worked with two or more stakes; the principle is exactly the same.

Trimming trac borders: This must be done very carefully otherwise the border will unravel. Make sure that you cut each end to rest on a stake.

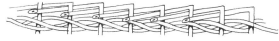

Trimming the stakes of a simple trac border

Madeira border

A Madeira border is the term used to describe a two- (or more) stake trac border forming the sides of a basket – presumably because it is used a lot by the willow basket makers on Madeira. Kinked or bent willow rods spoil the appearance of a Madeira border so some skill with willow is necessary to do this well.

How it is done: Insert two or three stakes either side of the base sticks when you are staking-up. It is not necessary to work an upsett if you are using this method, but if you do, treat the group of stakes as one. Work the trac, leaving the ends on the outside of the basket, and finish it by taking these over the next set of ends to the right and through to the inside.

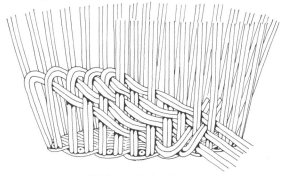

Working a Madeira border

Padded trac

This is an attractive border, with a smooth, rope-like appearance. It is very similar in method to the padded wale.

How it is done: If using **cane**, first squeeze all the stakes just above the weaving with round-nosed pliers. Prepare a core in exactly the same manner as for padded waling (see page 42). Lay it in front of the stakes, bend a stake forward over it and then back inside under the core two or more stakes to the right. Continue in this manner all the way round. When you get back to the beginning, overlap the ends as for padded waling. If the core is still visible and you want to cover it, you can do so, provided the ends are long enough, by working them over the core again. Whether you have worked the ends again or not, those on the inside need to be finished off to hold the whole thing together. This can be done either by threading them back to the outside under the border and cutting the ends carefully to rest against a stake, or by working a follow-on trac border on the inside (see page 75).

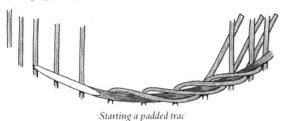

Starting a padded trac

Working the weavers a second time to cover the core

I have never tried a padded trac border in **willow**, but I see no reason why it should not work, provided you have a regular-sized core and kink all the stakes close to the top of the weaving first.

Rod Borders

These are strong and attractive, having an appearance somewhere between the padded trac and a plait. I tend to use variations of rod borders most of the time. Follow-on borders can be worked either into the border or under it to vary the appearance.

Like wales they can be worked using from two to six rods, though, also like wales, the bigger the number of rods, the stouter the material needs to be or the closer the stakes must be, otherwise the border will tend to be loose. The principle is the same for any number of rods.

Two-rod border

This requires a minimum length of stake equal to five times the distance between each stake.

How it is done: If using **cane**, first squeeze all the stakes 3 mm (⅛ in) from the weaving (I find that the fattest part of round-nosed pliers rested on top of the work determines about the right height). Take a stake, bend it down behind the next one to the right, and bring the end out to the front. With the second stake, repeat the process, taking it behind the third stake. Now go back and pick up the end of the first stake which is lying down, take it in front of the third stake, behind the fourth, and out to the front. Bend the third stake down to lie behind this. The two canes should be lying flat on the weaving and side by side. Now pick up the second stake which is lying down, take it in front of the fourth and behind the fifth. Lay the fourth stake down behind it, so that they are side by side. You will now have pairs of ends lying down; from now on use only the right-hand stake of the left-hand pair.

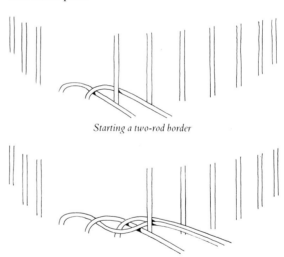

Starting a two-rod border

Picking up the first stake and laying down the third

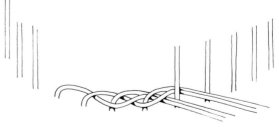

Picking up the second stake and laying down the fourth

Continue in this way until you get back to the point where you have one stake left standing. Working in the same pattern, take the next end from the front and thread it from the back to the front under the first stake, which now forms a loop. Take the last upright stake and thread it through the same loop behind the stake you have just worked. You will still have two pairs of stakes. Pick up the third stake from the right and take it under the loop formed by the second stake at the beginning, threading it from the back to the front, but over the cane already there so that it lies in front of it. Pick up the right-hand end of the last pair and do the same with it, taking it under the next loop (which now has two stakes forming it) and over the cane already there, to lie to the front of it.

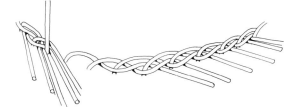

Two-rod border with one stake left standing

Working the picked-up stake and the last upright

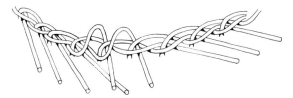

Threading the last two picked-up rods into place

The ends will now all be sticking out to the front. To get them back to the inside, either thread them through under the border, or work a follow-on border on the outside, or just trim them flush with the border.

If using **willow** the start of a two-rod border is exactly the same as for cane, except that it is necessary to kink only the first few rods. After that, you can kink them just prior to using them, as the correct height for the kink will have been established by the previous rods.

Cramming-off: When finishing rod borders in willow a technique known as cramming-off is often used. This avoids trying to thread the rods in and out of small spaces, which is guaranteed to result in badly kinked rods. However, I try not to use cramming-off, if at all possible, because no matter how well it is done, it never looks exactly the same as if the ends had been threaded into

place. It also tends to make the border narrower at that point. This can be hidden by a handle or a lid, but if you are not going to have either, it is difficult to decide where to start/cram-off the border so that it is as inconspicuous as possible. Cramming-off also prevents you from working any follow-on borders because it leaves no ends at that point with which to work them.

Nevertheless, you may find it helpful to know how to use this technique. When you reach the stage where one stake is left standing, thread it into its correct position. In order to do this without it kinking, however, it is necessary to 'soften' the rod a bit first by running it from butt to tip between your thumb and index finger, applying quite a lot of pressure.

Then, continuing the pattern, pick up the next rod from the front and kink it just before the next stake along. Cut a slype on the rod 5–8 cm (2–3⅛ in) – more on a very large basket – beyond the bend. Push the slype down into the channel to the left of the adjacent stake and tap it into place with a rapping iron or the handle of a bodkin. Do the same with the other two ends beside the subsequent stakes. This is easier to do on a bigger rod border, like a three- or four-rod one.

Putting the first cram into place

Putting the second and third crams into place

If you want to try finishing a willow border without cramming-off, then 'soften' all the rods involved in the manner already described and thread them carefully into place in the same manner as for cane.

Finishing rod borders: When trying to describe the finish of a border it tends to sound as though you have to perform some special ritual! If you bear in mind the following points you should be

Left: *Willow and painted veneer basket with four-rod behind two border; height c. 50 cm (19¼ in)*

able to finish any border without getting too knotted up:

1 Your aim is to make the pattern continuous. Look at a section of finished border very carefully and describe, verbally, what you see. Are the rods lying together or singly? What shape is the border? How far does each rod travel? Then try to match the ending with the rest of the border.
2 Rod borders are not finished as long as there are any pairs of rods left lying on the outside of the work.
3 If you do not seem to have enough rods left to finish the border, check back on the completed part to see if you have left a rod behind. In that case there will be a pair of ends somewhere and you will have to undo the border to that point and rework it.

Three- to six-rod borders

These follow the same principles as the two-rod border already described. Points to remember are:

a) You put down the required number of rods (i.e., three for a three-rod, four for a four-rod) at the beginning before picking up any from the front.
b) When you pick up the ones from the front the first three, four, five, etc., will be singles, but after that they will be in pairs. Pick up only the right-hand stake of the left-hand pair, unless it is damaged or a different size (willow), in which case, use the left-hand one.
c) Only two movements are involved – picking up and weaving with a stake from the front, and laying down a stake behind it.

Three- to six-rod behind two borders

These borders are very useful where the stakes are close together because they do not need to be bent as sharply as for the standard rod borders.

How they are done: Start in the same manner as for an ordinary rod border but instead of laying

each stake down behind one stake, lay them down behind two. When a stake is picked up from the front it must be taken in front of two uprights, instead of one, and then behind the next. Both the upright stake and the picked up one will eventually come out in the same place.

I use a four-rod behind two border a lot when working in willow. Finishing these borders is slightly trickier than the standard rod borders, but the same guidelines apply and the most important thing to do is look at the completed part of the border very carefully and aim to reproduce that.

Four-rod behind two border

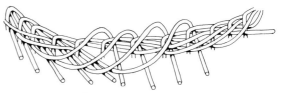

Finishing a four-rod behind two border

Rod borders – square work

All borders can be worked in the normal manner on square work, but they will tend to round the corners of the basket. With rod borders the sequence can be altered at the corners to keep them square. The technique is done differently depending on whether it is a blunt or a true corner.

Three-rod blunt corner – how it is done: Work a normal three-rod until you reach the corner and have one pair of stakes in the corner space and two pairs sticking out at the front. Take the next stake from the front (the right-hand stake of the left-hand pair) and lay it across the other pair, but do not bend the upright down. Pick up the next stake at the front and pull it round to lie just in front of the last one. You now have two stakes lying down either side of the left-hand corner stake. Take the last stake that you used and bend it over the other stakes, then behind the first upright on the next side of the basket. Lay the last upright stake on the first side down behind it. Pick up the end immediately to the right of the bent stake that formed the corner and work it as normal, but push it back into the corner, rather than pulling it away. Lay the next upright down behind it. You now have three pairs at the front and can continue as normal. This looks best when the two corner stakes are fairly close together.

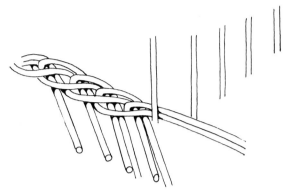

Starting point for a three-rod blunt corner

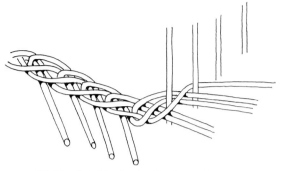

Working the left-hand stake of the three at the corner

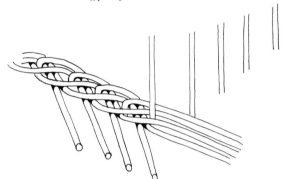

Four stakes at the corner space

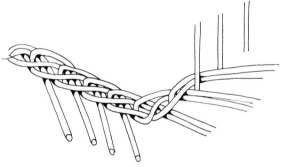

Laying down the first upright on the second side

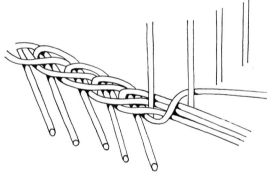

Working the left-hand stake of the four at the corner

Three-rod true corner – how it is done: If you have used a stout corner post for your basket you will need to put in a stake the same size as the rest to work the border. This can be pierced into the top of the post or put down to one side of it. Alternatively, two stakes can be put in, one either side of the corner post, and the corner can be worked as already described for a blunt corner.

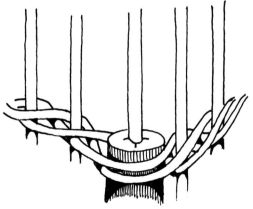

Corner stake pierced into the corner post

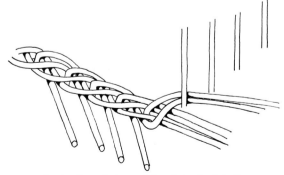

Laying down the last upright stake on the first side

(Continued overleaf)

If you use a single corner stake, work as normal until you have two pairs of stakes to the left of the corner post and one to the right. Take the next stake from the front and lay it in front of the corner post. Do not put the upright down. Then pick up the next stake and bend it up sharply, twisting it at the same time to prevent it cracking, and take it over the other ends, in front of the corner stake and behind the next upright stake.

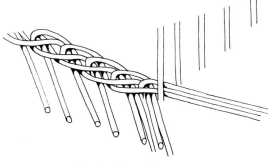

Starting a three-rod true corner

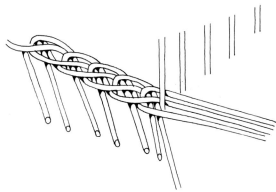

Working the next stake from the front

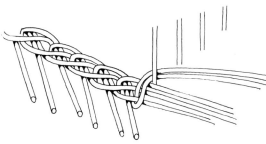

Bending up the last stake from the front

Lay the corner stake down behind the one you have just worked. Now pick up the stake sticking out at the corner, work it in front of a stake and behind a stake, then put the upright down behind it. You now have three pairs of stakes sticking out at the front. Next pick up the stake on the left, instead of its pair, as this tends to create less of a gap at the corner, and continue as normal. The remaining stake is left to be trimmed later.

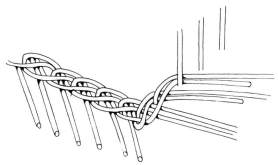

Working the stake sticking out at the corner

The same principle can be applied to all the other rod borders, gathering the stakes at the corner, folding one of them over all the others, and sorting out what is left to create as tidy an edge as possible.

Stopped rod border

This is a non-continuous border such as you might find on the ends of a square lid. It can also be used anywhere where you want to border only some of the stakes.

Three-rod stopped border for a lid – how it is done: Leave the corner sticks on the lid long, but trim all the others flush with the weaving. With the underside of the lid towards you, stake-up in the following manner. Put one stake in front of the left-hand outside stick or pair of sticks, one stake to the right of them, and then one stake to the left of each of the remaining sticks, except the outside ones at the other end.

Take another rod which is slightly longer than the other stakes and loop it around the outside sticks on the left, leaving the left-hand end just long enough to reach the fourth stake to the right. Bend or kink down the stake in front of the outside sticks.

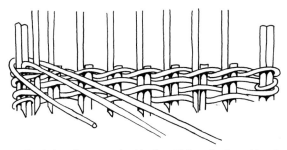

Lid staked-up for a stopped rod border with looped stake positioned

Take the left-hand short end of the loop in front of the outside sticks, over the bent stake, and behind the second stake along. Bend the stake to the left of it down behind it in the same way as for an ordinary rod border.

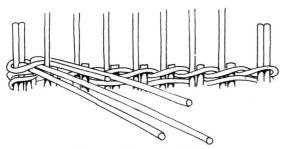

First stage of a stopped rod border

Now pick up the stake that was put in front of the outside sticks and take it in front of the first stake and behind the next. Take the upright on the left down behind it.

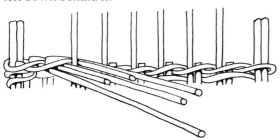

Second stage of a stopped rod border

Pick up the right-hand end of the loop and work in the same way, continuing with the three-rod border until you have two stakes left standing. Pick up the next stake from the front and take it in front of the first and behind the second stake.

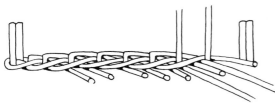

Preparing to finish a stopped rod border

Then, instead of putting the first stake down behind it, leave it upright and pick up the next one from the front. Take this in front of the second stake and behind and around the outside sticks, back to the front. Then take it through to the back to the right of the stake in that space and under itself. Put a bodkin into the left of the stake still standing on the left and pull the stake out. Cram down the end that you have just used to replace it.

Replacing the first stake removed

At the front you now have one pair left. Take the right-hand stake of the pair in front of the outside sticks, around the back, and as before cram it down where the second stake was.

Replacing the second stake removed

Trim the stick ends flush and either pin the top row to the outside sticks or make a couple of decorative bindings, lashing the border onto the weaving so there is no danger of it being pulled off.

Alternative ways of fixing the border

Rope Borders

Rope borders require a minimum length of stake equal to six times the distance between each stake. They can be worked in cane or willow. To achieve a successful rope border be sure to make the amount of twist regular so that each bunch of stakes looks the same; avoid kinking willow rods; and pick up the right stakes each time so as to maintain the twist.

Three-rod rope border

This can be used wherever you might use a standard rod border.

How it is done: Put in two extra stakes to the right of three stakes. Twist the left-hand bunch of three away from you two or more times (depending on how far apart the stakes are and how fine the material is). Then take the bunch in front of the next two stakes to the right and lay it down, leaving the ends at the back.

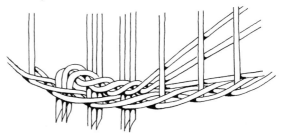

First stage of a three-rod rope border

Do the same with the next two bunches of stakes. As the fourth stake is a single it is necessary to pick up the two longest ends immediately behind it to make another bunch to twist. Pick these up so that the one being left behind remains underneath them, rather than sticking out at the top of the border. Check that as you pick them up, you do not unravel part of the twist.

Continue like this until you get back to the beginning. If you are working with cane, undo and pull out the stakes that you added at the start and replace them with the ones that you now have there, being careful to keep the border looking the same. If you are using willow it is easier to thread the last bunch of three through and then either cut off the extra stakes or thread them away into the body of the basket under the border.

Rope borders can be made bigger by starting with more stakes and working them in front of three or more.

Plait Borders

As the name suggests, these look like a plait or braid. They make a very strong visual feature and for that reason I think they should be used with caution, as they can easily overpower an otherwise subtle piece of work. The simplest is a three-pair plait, but like wales and rod borders you can work plaits with between four and seven pairs.

I do not like kinked willow rods on a border and particularly on a plait border, where they seem to jump out and wave at you. It is not always possible to avoid kinking rods, but the less tightly you try to make them turn, the better your chances are of avoiding kinks. So, if you are going to work a plait it will be easier if your stakes are not too close together; if they are, it would probably be better to work a four- (or more) pair plait. There are slight differences in the way plait borders are started and finished with cane and willow.

Left: *Detail showing a rope border in cane*

Right: *Linen basket in willow and painted card with a plait border; height c. 65 cm (25½ in)*

Three-pair plait

This requires a minimum length of stake equal to eight times the distance between each stake.

How it is done: If using **cane**, cut three extra stakes the same length and thickness as the original ones but preferably of a different colour to make them easier to see. These will be removed later. Also, cut two short, fat sticks 5 cm (2 in) long, which will be used as spacers. Squeeze all the stakes just above the weaving, using the fattest part of round-nosed pliers.

Put one of the spacers in between two stakes. Bend down over it the stake to the left of the spacer. Lay one of the spare stakes behind it. Then put the other spacer in the next space to the right over the top of the two stakes just laid down. Lay the stake to the left of it down over it and put another spare stake behind it. Now take the first pair and lay it over these two, in between the next two uprights. Bend the left-hand upright down over them and put the third spare stake behind it.

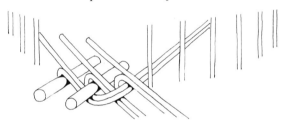

First stage of a three-pair plait

Take the left-hand pair at the front and put it in between the next two uprights. Pick up the left-hand pair at the back and bring it through to the front together with the stake that it is behind.

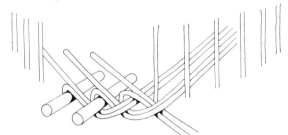

Second stage of a three-pair plait

Third stage of a three-pair plait

Take the left-hand pair through to the back over the three and in between the next two stakes. Take the left-hand pair at the back and bring it through to the front with the upright that it is behind.

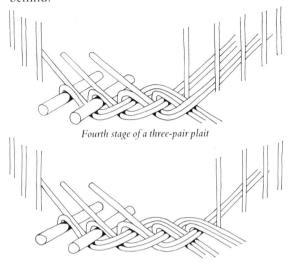

Fourth stage of a three-pair plait

Fifth stage of a three-pair plait

Now you will have two sets of three at the front and a pair at the back. From now on, pick up the two on the left of each group of three, leaving the right-hand one sticking out at the front. Continue in the same manner, until you have no more uprights left, working these two movements: pick up two from the front and lay them to the back; pick up three from the back and lay them to the front.

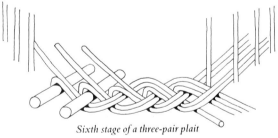

Sixth stage of a three-pair plait

Now remove the spacers and the three spare stakes – unthread them by pushing on the ends until you have a loop you can pull. This will leave you with space to thread the ends into. Take the next two from the front and thread them under the loop formed by the first stake. Then, because it is easier to see what is happening, instead of taking the two from the back, take the next two from the front and thread them over the first stake and under the second to the back. You now have three pairs at the back and it should be fairly apparent where these are threaded. Make sure there is an end sticking out of every space on the outside because only then will the border be finished.

Three-pair plait with spacers and spare stakes removed

Three pairs threaded to the back

Once you have got the hang of this border you will find that it is not necessary to put in the spare stakes; instead, simply leave the start loose. However, if you would rather have the ends on the inside, you will need to put two spare stakes to each original stake at the start, then as you work the border pick up all three from the front and drop the short one at the back instead of at the front. This will make a wider border.

Starting a three-pair plait with ends at the back

If using **willow** the extra stakes that you put in at the beginning remain, so choose three that are of a slightly smaller size than the stakes. Kink the first three stakes at a height above the weaving equal to the thickness of the stakes. Start in the same manner as for cane, leaving about 10 cm (4 in) of the spare stakes sticking out at the back. Work as for cane until you get back to the beginning. Then thread the two pairs from the front into place, again as for cane, which will leave you with three pairs at the back pointing to the right and three butt ends pointing to the left. Pull the pairs of ends to the left and thread the butts through to the right of them underneath the border. Then thread the right-hand one of each pair at the back down to the front and cut off all the ends flush with the border.

Finishing a plait border in willow

Follow-on Borders

These are borders worked with any remaining stakes after the main border has been completed. They can be as simple as threading the ends over or under the next one to the right, then through to the inside of the basket under the border; or they can be as complicated as a plait worked on the side of the basket. You can work as many follow-on borders as the remaining length of stake will allow.

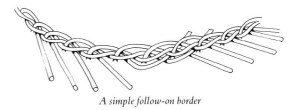

A simple follow-on border

Foot Borders

A foot is a border put onto the base of the basket. It is usually worked after the basket has been completed and any of the borders I have already described are suitable.

If using **willow** you can use the tops of the rods which are cut off after the main border has been worked. These are then slyped and inserted up through the waling beside the stakes or into the base and pricked down.

If using **cane** the same method can be applied or alternatively a foot border can be worked using the bye-stakes. In this case, cut the bye-stakes longer to allow for the border and put them in after only a couple of rows of waling. Use a bodkin to make a space and push them up through the waling from beneath the basket. Leave a long enough end on the underside to work the foot border, which will then have to be done straight away so that you can stand the basket on the work surface.

Handles

Handles come in many shapes and sizes but usually divide into three categories: cross handles, side handles and small or decorative handles. Cross handles are those which span the basket from one side to the other, as found on shopping baskets, for example. Side handles are usually just the right size to fit your hand into, and they are often found in pairs, one on either side of a basket. Sometimes tiny handles are found on lids or used as punctuation marks on small baskets; I call these small or decorative handles. They are not necessarily essential to function.

I find that the use of a particular handle – its scale and form – can make a very big difference to the overall appearance of a basket. The wrong sort of handle, of the wrong size or in the wrong place, can ruin an otherwise respectable piece of work. So they deserve as much attention as the rest of the basket.

On a basket that is to be carried, consideration should be given to:

a) The comfort of the handle when the basket is full.
b) The height of the handle above the basket – will the length of handle result in the basket trailing on the ground?
c) Whether or not it will be strong enough. The strength of a handle is generally determined by how well it is fastened onto the basket, because that is the point at which it will usually give way first.

Cross Handles

These are generally made using a handle bow. This is a stout cane or willow rod used to form the handle, which is usually then covered. (Ash or hazel rods can also be used instead of willow.) Two or three bows can be inserted side by side to create a wide, flat handle.

Above: *Willow and plastic sheet oval shopping basket with roped cross handle; height c. 46 cm (18 in)*

If it is to be a fairly hefty handle, it is a good idea to insert handle liners as you weave the sides of the basket. These are made out of material the same thickness as the handle bow and each has a slype on one end. Cut the handle liners long enough for you to be able to grasp them easily in order to pull them out after the border has been worked. The resulting space for the bow to slide into is known as a bow mark. Handle liners are not essential for lightweight handles.

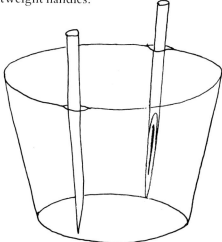

Handle liners in position

The handle bow is slyped at either end so that the cut side will be on the inside of the basket, and it is then pushed as far down into the sides as possible. The use of a bodkin and tallow or soap will generally do the job, but the work can be distorted by doing this. With willow it is usually a good idea to soak the handle bow, tie it into shape and leave it to dry before using it. This prevents it from distorting the basket. The bow is then either roped or wrapped.

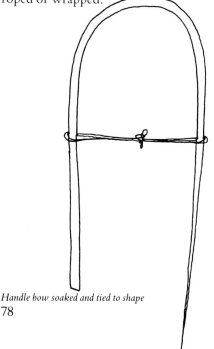

Handle bow soaked and tied to shape

78

Roped cross handles

If using **cane** a roped handle looks particularly good in coloured material.

How it is done: Insert a handle bow and fasten it in place by putting a tack through the top waling and into the bow on the inside of the basket (this is really only a fail-safe device because a well-roped handle should not pull out). Take three or four long canes (depending on how fat your handle bow is) four and a half times the length of the handle bow. Put them through the basket from the outside to the inside, to the left of the handle bow and just under or in any top waling. The ends on the inside should be one and a half times as long as the handle bow. Take the outside ends up to the right-hand side of the bow and wind them around it three or four times – depending on the length of bow – leaving equally spaced gaps between the groups of cane.

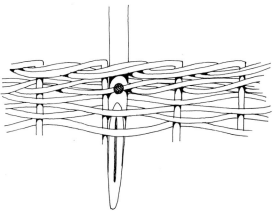

Position of the tack

On reaching the other side, take the ends across the bow and under or into the top wale from the outside to the inside in exactly the same manner as when you started (both ends of the handle should look identical). Bring the ends of cane back up to the left-hand side of the bow and wind them across the handle, starting above the first set of canes. When you reach the other side, leave the ends on the inside. Pick up the ends you left at the beginning, bring them up to the left of the handle and work them back over to the other side, filling in the small gaps (known as grins). If you find this fails to fill them in, then put a single cane down beside the handle bow, wherever the gap is, wind it around the handle, and push the other end down beside the bow.

A binding is now put around each end to hold everything in place. Insert a length of the same cane to the right of the handle bow, bring it to the front, and wind it as tightly as possible around the handle five or six times. Hold the loose ends in and pull the canes coming up at the back of the handle tightly into the bow. The end is then threaded down under the wraps, following the line of the canes already roped round the handle. It is pulled tight and cut off flush. The ends on the inside are cut so that they rest on the border.

If using **willow** the handle bow is inserted in the same manner. Choose eight or ten rods (depending on the size of the handle bow), which are one and a half to two times the length of the bow. Slype four or five rods and put them into the border to the left of the handle bow on each side. Take one group and wind it carefully (to avoid kinking) around the bow three or four times, leading with the tips when threading through under the handle and leaving equally sized gaps between the groups. When you reach the other side, leave the ends on the inside. Take the other set and work it over to the other side, starting the wraps below the set already in place.

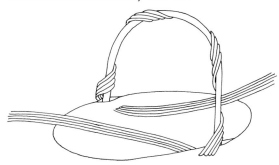

First crossing of a roped handle

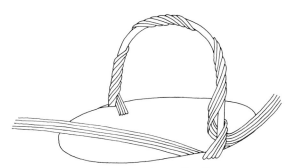

Second crossing of a roped handle

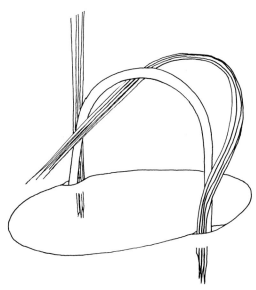

Two sets of willow rods inserted to the left of the handle bow on each side

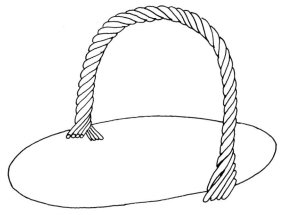

Completed roped handle

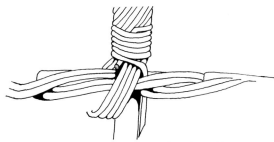

Binding on the handle seen from the outside

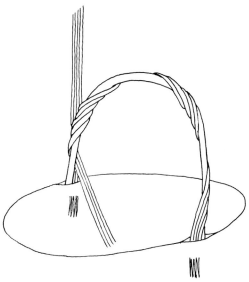

First set wound around the bow

If there are still gaps in the rope, add an extra stake or stakes, slyped and put in beside the bow in a convenient place. It may be that there are gaps on the top of the bow but not underneath, which is likely because the top is longer. In this case you will be unable to fit in any more rods and the best thing to do is try to spread the rods on the top more evenly.

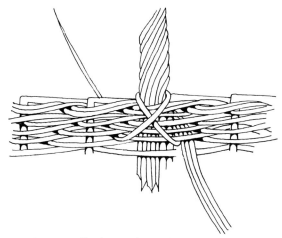

First stage of binding, working each strand individually

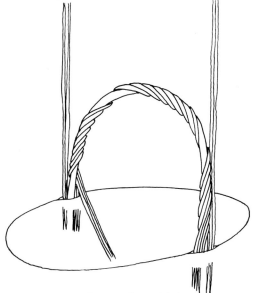

Second set wound around the bow

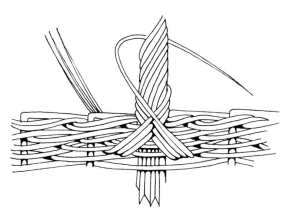

Nearly completed binding

Once the gaps have been eliminated, the ends on both sides are threaded carefully from the inside to the outside to the right of the handle bow, making sure that they do not cross over each other. The tips which are sticking out to the right of the handle at the front are now taken either individually or as a bunch diagonally up to the left of the bow, round the back of it, and then diagonally down to the left and underneath the wale, where they are threaded back to the inside. The tips are then divided into two bunches and woven away to left and right.

Wrapped cross handles

A wrapped handle can be worked using flat-band or lapping cane, skeined willow, plastic tape, etc. Anything that is flat and will be comfortable to hold when carrying the basket laden is suitable.

How it is done: The bow or bows are inserted in the same manner as for a roped handle. Take a piece of wrapping material at least four times the length of the bow. Thread an end of the wrapping material from the outside to the inside of the basket, to the right of the handle bow and under the wale, until there is approximately 15 cm (6 in) on the inside. Bring this end up over the border and cross it diagonally to the left of the bow, where it is taken through to the inside again and brought up to lie behind the handle. Now take the long end diagonally up to the left of the handle bow, so making a cross on the outside of the basket, and then wrap it tightly around the bow until you reach the other side of the basket. Next, take it diagonally across the bow on the outside

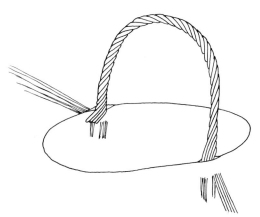

Ends threaded to the outside of the basket

under the border, then up over the border on the same side of the bow and diagonally down to the right, threading the end back to the inside. The end is then brought up on the inside and tucked down into the border using a bodkin.

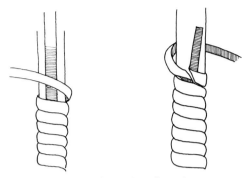

Inserting a new skein and completing the join

The wrap described here is a very simple one which can be made more interesting by working extra strands in with it and taking the wrapping over and under these. The strands can be left to run straight or can cross over or twist around each other. Patterns created like this are generally known as leader patterns.

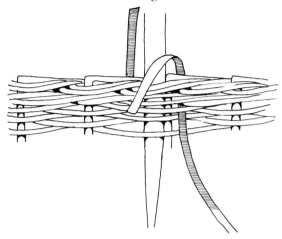

Starting a wrapped handle

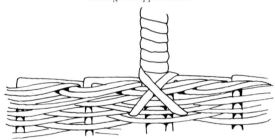

The decorative cross of a wrapped handle

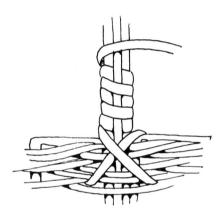

Wrapped handle with an extra decorative strand

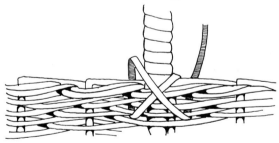

Completing a wrapped handle

If you are using willow it will probably be necessary to join skeins at some point. When the piece of wrapping material is within eight or so wraps from its end, lay a new piece in at the back of the handle, wrong side up. Wind over it four or five times and then on the underside of the handle, fold the old end so that it lies wrong side up against the handle. Fold the new end out and start winding with it. This makes a neat mitred join.

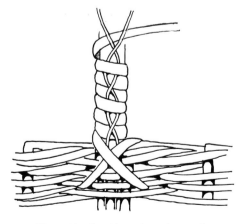

Wrapped handle with two decorative strands

Make sure to tack these handles carefully, as they are only as secure as the strength of the wrapping material.

Side Handles

These can be done in any of the ways already described, the only difference being that smaller handle bows are used.

Twisted handles can also be worked, either with a single strand or a double one. They can be done in cane or willow, but before attempting them in willow it is necessary to twist the rod to break down the fibres a bit, which prevents it from kinking. This is a knack and you will probably find you demolish a few rods before you get one that is usable.

To twist a willow rod, insert it into the basket so that it is held firmly. Hold the rod loosely with your left hand and, using your right hand and starting at the tip of the rod, roll it between thumb and forefinger away from you. You will feel the fibres give as you do this. Gradually move both hands down the rod, twisting the rod all the way down. After you have gone about a quarter of the way down the rod, it is possible to begin a cranking movement. Provided the rod is well twisted to start with, your right arm can start to make gradually wider circles, while your left hand continues to hold the rod. The rod can split lengthways as you are doing this but you do not need to worry too much about this as long as all the pith does not fall out. If it does, however, it will probably be better to use a fresh rod.

Single-rod twisted handle

This can be done in cane or willow.

How it is done: If using **cane**, mark the position of both ends of the handle and, working from the outside of the basket, insert the cane down into the border beside a stake at the right-hand end of the intended handle. Bend the cane over to the left, making a loop no more than three fingers high in the centre. Take the end through from the outside to the inside under the border at the left-hand mark. Loosely wind the end clockwise back to the right-hand end of the handle and take the cane through from the outside to the inside to the left of where the original stake was inserted. Bring the end back up under the bow, and then take it round the bow clockwise to the left in the spaces between the two previous wraps. When you get back to the other side, thread the end down into the space beside the stake.

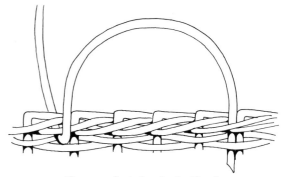

First stage of a single-rod twisted handle

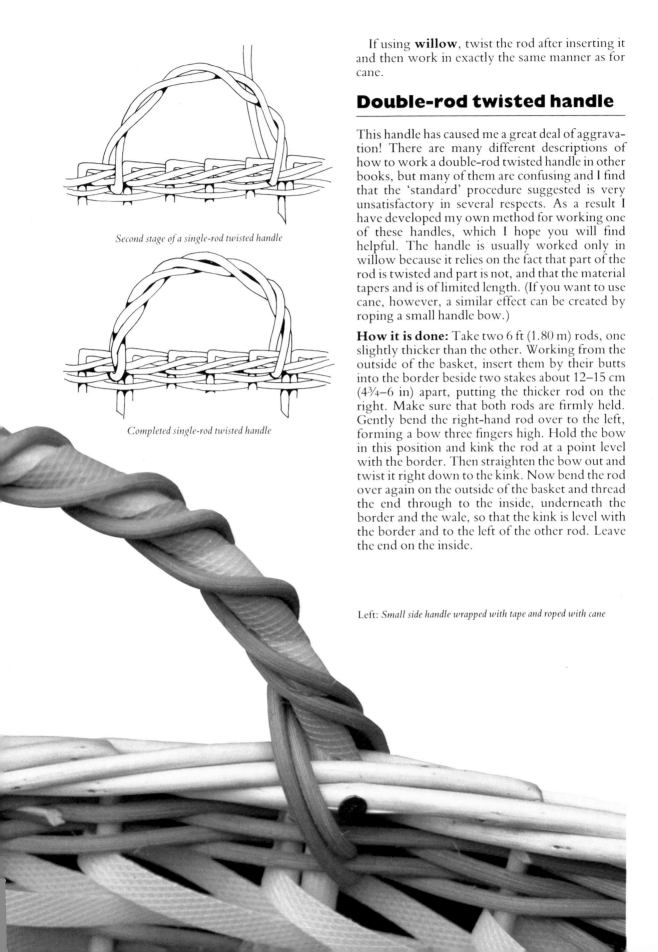

Second stage of a single-rod twisted handle

Completed single-rod twisted handle

Left: Small side handle wrapped with tape and roped with cane

If using **willow**, twist the rod after inserting it and then work in exactly the same manner as for cane.

Double-rod twisted handle

This handle has caused me a great deal of aggravation! There are many different descriptions of how to work a double-rod twisted handle in other books, but many of them are confusing and I find that the 'standard' procedure suggested is very unsatisfactory in several respects. As a result I have developed my own method for working one of these handles, which I hope you will find helpful. The handle is usually worked only in willow because it relies on the fact that part of the rod is twisted and part is not, and that the material tapers and is of limited length. (If you want to use cane, however, a similar effect can be created by roping a small handle bow.)

How it is done: Take two 6 ft (1.80 m) rods, one slightly thicker than the other. Working from the outside of the basket, insert them by their butts into the border beside two stakes about 12–15 cm (4¾–6 in) apart, putting the thicker rod on the right. Make sure that both rods are firmly held. Gently bend the right-hand rod over to the left, forming a bow three fingers high. Hold the bow in this position and kink the rod at a point level with the border. Then straighten the bow out and twist it right down to the kink. Now bend the rod over again on the outside of the basket and thread the end through to the inside, underneath the border and the wale, so that the kink is level with the border and to the left of the other rod. Leave the end on the inside.

Next, twist up the second rod and bring it forwards over the bow and through it to the inside. Wind around the bow three times and then thread it from the outside to the inside immediately under the border and to the right of the first stake. Bring the end up inside the handle and wind it around the bow from right to left, in between the previous wraps. Then take it from the outside to the inside to the left of the bow and also immediately under the border. The end is brought up to the outside of the bow and wound around to the right underneath the first wrap. On reaching the right-hand side, take it from the outside to the inside but a row of waling lower down than the previous one. The end is then left on the inside.

Now go back to the left-hand side and pick up the end of the original handle bow, bring it up to the outside of the handle and wind it across to the right, running it in between the second and third wraps. When it reaches the right-hand end, take it through from the outside to the inside, one row lower down than the other two and level with the lowest one at the left-hand end. Bring the end up at the back and work it back over to the left in between the first and second wraps. When it reaches the other side it is taken through diagonally under the border in between the other two already there so that it comes out on the handle side of them. The ends on the inside are then tucked up under the other two ends and cut off.

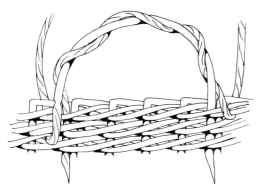

First and second stages of a double-rod twisted handle

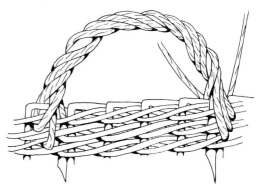

Fifth stage of a double-rod twisted handle

Third stage of a double-rod twisted handle

Completed double-rod twisted handle

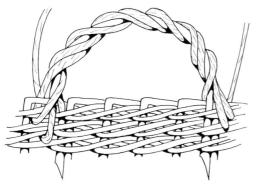

Fourth stage of a double-rod twisted handle

Small or Decorative Handles

These can be tiny versions of any of the handles already described, or they can be small rings or plaits – or even other things altogether like leather, beads, carved wood, bones and shells.

Right: *Cane wastepaper basket with a small roped handle used as a decorative feature; height c. 35 cm (13¾ in)*

Making a cane ring

Take a length of cane and tie a knot so that the short end sticks out on one side and the long end on the other. Pull the ring to the desired size. Thread the long end in and out of the loop, in the manner used when making handles, as many times as is necessary for the size of the ring. Then work it around once more, following the grooves made by the previous wraps. The end is then either cut at the point where the short end was left or used to fasten the ring onto the basket.

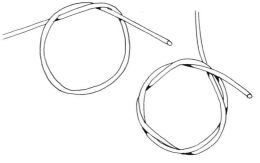

Above: *Making a cane ring*

Finishing Touches

These are things that may be essential to the proper functioning of your basket but which take relatively little of the material that goes into the making of the whole piece. It is all too easy, therefore, to regard them as not very important and as a job to be left until some point in the future when you have a few minutes to spare.

In practice, finishing touches usually take quite a long time to do well. It is worth giving thought to this in your overall scheme because a lid, hinge or catch can be the focal point on the entire basket. Finishing touches also allow you the opportunity to add something different to your basket that will make it unique.

Lids

Lids are the bane of my basket-making life and I try to avoid them whenever possible! However, I learnt quickly that people do not want to see their dirty laundry. . . . So, I use a few methods for making lids that do not require spending an inordinate amount of time trying to get them to fit.

Lids work in three ways: they either drop on top of the basket; or they drop into it to rest on a ledge; or they fit over the top of the basket.

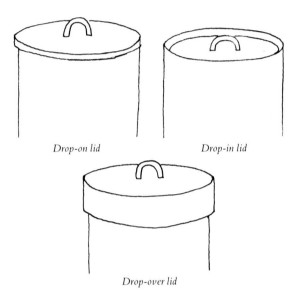

Drop-on lid   *Drop-in lid*

Drop-over lid

Drop-on lids

These often sit flush on top of the basket, can be flat or slightly domed, and can be hinged to stay in place when you lift them; or sometimes they have a rim underneath the lid to locate it.

Drop-on lid with a locating rim

Drop-on lids are made using the same technique that you employed to work the base of the basket. The lid may be a different size from the base, though, in which case you would need to adjust the quantity of sticks used in the slath. For round and oval lids, the sticks should be just a bit longer than the diameter of the basket.

You may choose to work the lid in a different weave from the one used for the base – perhaps to match it with the weave used on the sides of the basket. In this case, too, it may be necessary to alter the number of sticks used.

Generally, lids look better if the weaving is done with material the same size or slightly smaller than that used for the side weaving, because of the scale of the lid in relation to the rest of the basket. This means you may also need to use slightly smaller sticks than you used on the base.

How it is done: Weave the lid out to within 6–12 mm (¼–½ in) of the outside edge of the basket, depending on whether or not you are going to work a wale and on the type of border you plan to use. If you decide to work a wale, cut the stick ends flush with the weaving and stake-up in the same manner as for the base of a basket but using smaller material. Complete a row of waling, separating the stakes out evenly, then work your chosen border making sure that you know whether the ends will be on the top or the bottom of the lid.

A very wide plait can be used on the edge of a lid to act as a locater, but it works well only if your lid is near perfect size.

Round or oval lid with locating rim: The rim can either be worked into the lid or added afterwards.

a) *To work the rim into the lid:* Mark on your sticks the point at which you will need to work the rim so that it will just fit loosely inside the top edge of the basket. When you have woven out to these marks, work one row of five- or six-rod wale with the inside of the lid facing you. If you think that will not make a deep enough rim to hold the lid in place on the basket then work it as a padded wale. Alternatively, when you reach the marked point, put in short stakes either side of the lid sticks all the way round and bend them down at right angles to the lid sticks. Check that they are positioned in the right place by trying the lid on with the short stakes down inside the basket. Then continue weaving the lid. Work a trac border using the short stakes on the inside of the lid and check that the lid fits before going ahead and putting the edge border on. If the lid is too tight, try working the trac border again but this time more tightly.

b) *To add a rim afterwards:* This is one of the methods I prefer because it is quick and fairly easy to do accurately. Weave your lid first, then make a ring either out of handle cane or stout willow, big enough to fit just inside the rim of the basket. Cut slypes on the two ends and overlap them, holding them together with masking tape, which can be removed later, or fastening them with small pins. The completed circle is then laced onto the under-side of the lid, either through the weaving or around the sticks. The material you use for lacing must be strong and should be inconspicuous if it is visible on top of the lid. Lace tightly so that the two ends of the ring are held firmly together.

Locating rim laced onto the underside of a lid

Square drop-on lids: The trouble with these, particularly for beginners, is that unless your basket is a perfectly regular shape at the top, with right-angled corners and straight sides, it is very hard to make a lid which fits well. These lids are generally slightly easier to get to fit when made in willow rather than cane. It is also easier if you work a true, rather than blunt, corner on your basket if you are planning to put a lid on it. My advice, however, is that unless you have a reason-ably regular top to your square basket, or until you are more experienced in basket making, it may be better to reconsider whether it really needs a lid!

For those of you who want to have a go at making a square lid in cane or willow, you will need to use a screwblock in exactly the same way as for the base. Check the measurements first, though, because the top of your basket may well be narrower or wider than the original base. Try to mimic the outline of the top edge of your basket – if it narrows at one end, make the lid do the same. If the ends bulge, then do some packing at each end of the lid. On blunt-cornered baskets, make lid stakes curve in at the ends to try to match the shape. A lid that matches the basket will look much better (no matter how odd the shape) than a perfectly square lid on an unevenly shaped basket.

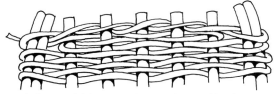

End of a square lid showing packing and shaping of the edge sticks

Right: *Cane drop-in lid for a linen basket; diameter c. 17 cm (6¾ in)*

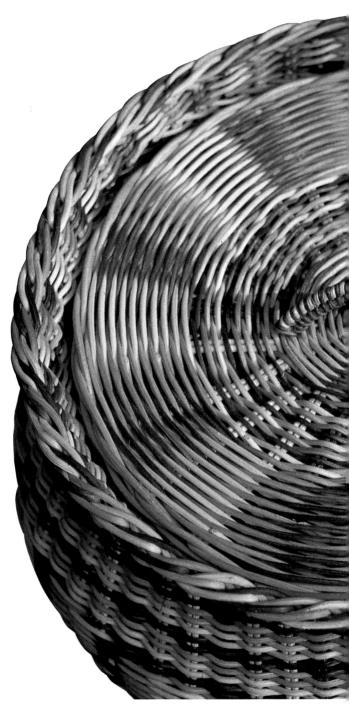

Make the lid as wide as the top edge of the basket, so that it fits flush, but slightly shorter by the amount you need to work a stopped border (see page 70) at each end. Stake-up for this and work it with the underside of the lid towards you.

Drop-in lids

These require a ledge to sit on inside the basket. The ledge can be made by one of three methods. The first requires that a five- or six-rod or padded wale is worked inside the basket at the point where you want the lid to rest. The second uses the bye-stakes in cane or extra stakes in willow that are bent into the basket at the point where the ledge is to be. A trac border is then worked with them in the same manner as for a drop-on lid. This is difficult to do in willow unless the stakes are quite fine or the basket is big, because you have to work the rods in a confined space. The third way to make the ledge is by shaping the basket sharply outwards at the point where the lid is to rest.

Ledge for a drop-in lid without a locating rim

Drop-in lid using the top of the basket turned sharply outwards as a ledge

For the first two methods to be satisfactory the lid must not be too much smaller than the basket, otherwise your wale or trac will need to be huge in order for the lid to reach it. A big ledge obviously restricts the amount of space inside the basket.

The lids themselves are made in the same manner as drop-on lids and can be flat (all shapes) or domed (round and oval only).

Drop-over lids

These are essentially upside-down baskets that either fit over the tops of other baskets or rest on a ledge outside the basket so that extra space can be created by deepening the lid.

It is fairly straightforward to make them fit over the basket. Just weave a base and stake-up in the normal manner, but make it a little bit bigger than the top of the basket. The trick is in getting this just the right amount bigger, so keep checking after you have upsett, because these lids often seem to come out either too big or so tight that they will not come off once rammed on.

The sort of lid that rests on an outside ledge is usually known as a trunk cover, and the ledge is made with a five- or six-rod or padded wale on the outside of the basket.

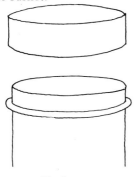

Trunk cover

Another sort of drop-over lid is made exactly the same diameter as the main basket so that it sits edge to edge. The lid is held in place by an upright fence worked around inside the main basket, using either bye-stakes or extra stakes added in. This fence can be woven and bordered or made as a large trac border, and it should come at least 3 cm (1¼ in) above the top edge of the basket.

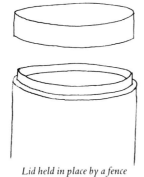

Lid held in place by a fence

With all drop-over lids, it is better to have the ends of the stakes on the outside, so that they do not catch as the lid is taken off and put on.

Hinges

These can be made out of any material so there is plenty of scope for inventiveness here. Leather, chair cane, metal clip rings and polypropylene cords, for example, all make good hinges.

A simple method, using cane or willow, is to loop a weaver around a stake on the outside of the basket just under the top wale. Twist the two ends together to make a rope, twisting the right-hand end away from you and crossing it over the other one to the left. Repeat this sequence, keeping the tension even. Thread the rope through the lid and bring the ends back through to the outside of the basket just under the top wale, one either side of the stake that the weaver is looped around. Weave the ends in and out of a couple of stakes, then cut them off.

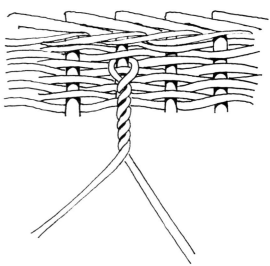

Twisting a loop of cane to make a hinge

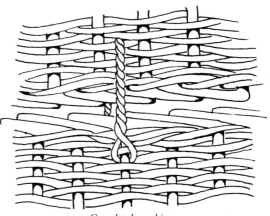

Completed cane hinge

Fastenings

Like hinges, these provide plenty of scope for your imagination. You can use many things – catches meant for leather handbags, buttons, beads, and so on – but a simple type to use for cane and willow baskets is a loop through a loop, held together with a peg.

Loop fastening – how it is done: Fasten a weaver onto either the top or the edge of the lid, looping it around a stake or the edge sticks of a square lid. Twist the two ends together for long enough to make a loop down onto the side of the basket. Allow the loop to twist over – it will usually do so of its own accord. At this point, where it crosses, thread one end through the two already twisted strands with a bodkin. Continue twisting the ends until you reach the lid, then weave them away into the lid so that they match the start.

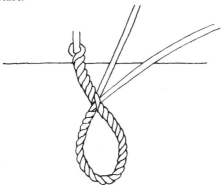

Making a loop for a loop and peg fastening

Make another smaller loop on the front of the basket to fit inside the first loop and at right angles to it. Cut a peg out of thick cane or willow, put a point on one end, and cut a groove around the other. Alternatively, a hole can be drilled through it, and either more cane or willow, or something else, made into a rope and used to tie it onto the basket so that it is not lost.

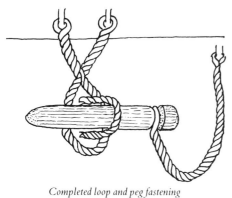

Completed loop and peg fastening

Singeing and Varnishing

Cane

Cane tends to leave little hairs sticking out on a finished basket, so prior to varnishing it is a good idea to singe them off. I have an ancient gas cooker with a wand for lighting the oven which produces a gentle blue flame that is perfect for the job. Anything that produces a blue flame will work, but do not use a candle or taper as these will leave black marks all over your work – although these might make an interesting decoration if done deliberately! The first time you try this technique, damp your basket first, as this will make sure you burn just the hairs and not the whole thing.

The dyes that I use are fairly colour-fast even in bright sunlight, but I always varnish my baskets anyway. I think varnishing guards against fading and I know that it prevents the cane from absorbing dirt, which means that with the odd brush and occasional wash a basket should stay looking as bright as when it was made. The varnish I use is a satin-finish polyurethane which has a slight sheen, but you can also get a high-gloss finish and a matt one that you won't even know is there. I don't however think that a matt varnish protects against fading as it absorbs rather than reflects light.

I apply the varnish with an electric airless sprayer (which doesn't destroy the ozone layer). If you have several baskets to varnish this method is a lot quicker than brushing it on, even taking into account the time spent setting up a spray booth, putting on the mask and overalls, and cleaning the equipment afterwards. Actually, I have to be honest and say that this is one of the few aspects of my basket making in which my husband gets involved (apart from the involuntary ones like having to move willows out of the bath in order to use it himself). It is much quicker to do spray varnishing with two people, so I line the baskets up and hang them on the line after he has sprayed them.

If you are making one basket at a time, however, the best way to varnish is with a brush. Whichever method you use, two coats of varnish are sufficient for most baskets.

Willow

Varnishing is sometimes done on willow baskets but it really isn't necessary. The willow develops a sheen of its own with use that is very attractive, though maybe varnish deters woodworm.

Design Calculations

Design, in whatever area, involves two main elements: the idea and the practicalities of carrying it out. I have already discussed the first of these, in relation to basket making, in the Introduction (see page 9), so this chapter deals solely with the practical aspects of design. In the exercises and examples included so far I have given details, where necessary, of how many sticks and stakes to use, but when you come to make your own baskets you will need to know how to decide these things for yourself.

Once you have shaken all your bits and pieces of inspiration into a single tangible idea you can start on the practicalities. These cover such questions as where you are going to start your basket, what shaped base it will have, and what materials and how many sticks and stakes are needed. It is usually fairly easy to decide on the shape and materials for the one tends to suggest the other; but determining the quantity of sticks and stakes requires some mathematics.

These calculations are hard work if you find mathematics difficult, as I do, but although it is possible in most cases to make a fairly accurate guess at the right number of sticks and stakes needed, being able to work out precise quantities mathematically is very useful in those instances when the widest part of the basket is a lot wider than the base.

Right: *Cane linen basket requiring precise calculation to create the pattern; height c. 70 cm (27½ in)*

Round bases

First decide on the measurement of the widest part of the basket. Using the material that you think you want for the stakes, determine how far apart you want these to be at the widest part of the basket (which need not necessarily be the top edge). Calculate the circumference of the basket at that point by multiplying the diameter by π (3.14). For example, if your basket is to have a diameter of 35 cm (13¾ in) at the widest point, following the formula C = D × π the calculation will be as follows:

$$35 \text{ cm} \times 3.14 = 110 \text{ cm}$$

The circumference of the basket at the widest point is therefore 110 cm (43¼ in). If you decided that your stakes were to be 2 cm (¾ in) apart at that point, you will need fifty-five stakes, the number resulting from the division of 110 by 2.

Each stick on the base of a round basket needs four stakes (two at each end), so you must divide 55 by 4 to determine the number of sticks required. This results in either thirteen or fourteen. Thirteen sticks will require fifty-two stakes and fourteen sticks will require fifty-six stakes. If you use fourteen sticks you would need to thread seven sticks through seven sticks, which would create quite a wide slath. To avoid that you could decide to make a smaller slath, in which case you would need to insert the extra stakes into the base either by putting more to each stick or by putting them in at a later stage. The important point to remember is that one way or another you must put in all fifty-five stakes.

Oval bases

If you are working an elliptical oval the same principle as for round baskets applies, but for an oblong oval the calculations are slightly different.

Remember that an oblong oval consists of two half circles joined by a straight piece in between. In order to determine the circumference at the widest point you therefore need to determine the circumference of the circle and add the length of the two straight sides. Take, as an example, a basket that you wish to be 30 cm (12 in) long and 14 cm (5½ in) wide at the widest point. The latter measurement is the diameter of the circle, so to calculate the circumference, apply the same formula as for a round basket: C = D × π. This will give you the following calculation:

$$14 \text{ cm} \times 3.14 = 44 \text{ cm}$$

To determine the length of each straight side, deduct the diameter of the circle from the overall length of the basket:

$$30 \text{ cm} - 14 \text{ cm} = 16 \text{ cm}$$

Therefore the total circumference of the basket at the widest point is equal to the circumference of the circle plus the lengths of the two sides:

$$44 \text{ cm} + 16 \text{ cm} + 16 \text{ cm} = 76 \text{ cm}$$

If you decided that your stakes were to be 2 cm (¾ in) apart, divide 76 by 2. The result will give you the number of stakes required: thirty-eight.

To determine how many long and how many short sticks are needed for thirty-eight stakes, remember again that the oval is made up of two half circles plus a straight section, and calculate accordingly. Treat the circle part as though it were a round basket and work out how many sticks you would need if you were making one of 44 cm (17½ in) circumference – i.e., with twenty-two stakes 2 cm (¾ in) apart. This number of stakes divided by 4, to ascertain the number of sticks required, results in either five or six; choose five so that you have fewer rather than more stakes to deal with at this stage – three sticks going the length of the basket and two short ones going across. Remember to separate the two halves of the circle by spreading the short sticks apart.

At this point you now have to determine how many more short sticks are required. Each end of the five sticks already cut takes two stakes, which accounts for twenty stakes. As you have already calculated that thirty-eight stakes are needed, this leaves eighteen more to be accommodated. On an oval base there are usually two sticks together at each end of the slath, both of which have two stakes at each end. By adding another one to each of the two stakes already in place, eight more stakes are used up. This leaves ten stakes to be placed and as the short sticks across the centre of an oval slath require only one stake at each end, this means that five short sticks will be needed.

Square bases

The calculations for square bases are easy because you can work out the number of stakes required by simply dividing the length of the sides by the planned distance between the stakes. You can then calculate the number of sticks needed.

Length of stakes (cane)

To determine the length of the stakes for your cane basket, add together: the amount to be pushed into the base (slightly less than the radius of the base); *plus* the finished height of the basket (making allowance for the shape); *plus* the border, the amount for which will depend on the type chosen, but 20–25 cm (8–9¾ in) allows for some uncertainty at this point; *plus* the follow-on border (if any); *plus* 2.5 cm (1 in) for errors, change of plan, etc.

Stake and Strand
Projects

Cane Bowls

These bowls are just the right size for a meagre fruit-eater or a greedy sweet-consumer and look good with fresh eggs nestling in them.

Finished measurements

Height: 7.5 cm (3 in)
Width at border: 23.5 cm (9¼ in)
Width of base: 13.5 cm (5¼ in)

Materials

Each bowl requires 100 g (3½ oz) cane:
  9 base sticks 16.5 cm (6½ in) long of 3.3 mm (No. 10) natural
  36 stakes 24 cm (9½ in) long of 3 mm (No. 8) natural
  Remainder of weight in 2.6 mm (No. 6) in three colours and natural for weaving

(NOTE: For American equivalents of cane sizes, see page 15.)

Tools

Side-cutters
Small/medium bodkin or awl
Round-nosed pliers
Flexible steel tape measure

Cane bowls

Instructions

Pierce five of the base sticks and thread the other four through. Using one of the weavers, *tie in the slath* with two rounds of *pairing*, treating each bunch of sticks as though it is a single stick. On the third row, separate the groups of four sticks into pairs and the groups of five sticks into a pair, a single and a pair. On the fifth row, separate all the sticks into singles. Continue pairing until the base measures 13.5 cm (5¼ in). Tuck away the ends of the weavers and trim the base sticks flush with the weaving.

Cut a point on one end of each of the thirty-six stakes and *stake-up*, putting one stake either side of each stick. Damp the stakes but do not squeeze them. Take three natural weavers and work three rounds of *three-rod waling*, *stepping-up* on each row

and shaping the basket upwards as you work. On the last row, cut two of the weavers immediately after the step-up and add two coloured weavers, each a different colour. Work seventeen rows of three-rod waling without stepping-up, changing one of the colours every so many rows. These patterns look best if you do not change colours too frequently.

Shape the work so that it measures 23 cm (9 in) across the top after seventeen rows. Damp and *squeeze* the stakes, then work a *three-rod behind two border*. *Trim* all the ends, *singe* any hairs and *varnish*.

Cane Table Mats

My students tend to groan if I mention table mats – they seem to have a poor image – but they provide a good opportunity to try out different patterns and can provide an interesting talking point between courses!

I have restricted myself here to two colours to give some unity to the set, as in other respects they are all different. If you are a patient perfectionist you could of course make four identical mats. I tried it once and found that I lost interest somewhere around the third row of the second one.

I have attempted to grade the mats according to difficulty, starting with the easiest, but really there is little to choose between them. I have deliberately kept all the joins at the back of the work except with the mats that are waled, so as not to disturb the pattern too much.

Finished measurements

Diameter of each mat: 25 cm (9¾ in)

Materials

Each mat requires 75 g (2½ oz) cane:

No. 1 12 base sticks 27 cm (10⅝ in) long of 3 mm (No. 8) natural
24 sticks 11.5 cm (4½ in) long of 3 mm (No. 8) natural
24 sticks 8 cm (3⅛ in) long of 3 mm (No. 8) natural
48 border stakes 19 cm (7½ in) long of 2.5 mm (No. 5) natural
Weavers of 2.5 mm (No. 5) in black and natural

No. 2 10 base sticks 27 cm (10⅝ in) long of 3 mm (No. 8) natural
20 sticks 11 cm (4⅜ in) long of 3 mm (No. 8) natural
40 border stakes 15 cm (6 in) long of 2.5 mm (No. 5) natural
Weavers of 2.5 mm (No. 5) in black and natural

No. 3 12 base sticks 27 cm (10⅝ in) long of 3 mm (No. 8) natural
24 sticks 11 cm (4⅜ in) long of 3 mm (No. 8) natural
52 border stakes 17 cm (6¾ in) long of 2.5 mm (No. 5) black
Weavers of 2.5 mm (No. 5) in black and natural

Left: *Cane table mats; No. 1* (top left), *No. 2* (bottom left), *No. 3* (top right) *and No. 4* (bottom right)

No. 4 12 base sticks 27 cm (10⅝ in) long of 3 mm (No. 8) natural
24 sticks 10 cm (4 in) long of 3 mm (No. 8) natural
48 border stakes 17 cm (6¾ in) long of 2.5 mm (No. 5) black
Weaver of 2 mm (No. 3) natural
Weavers of 2.5 mm (No. 5) in black and natural

(NOTE: For American equivalents of cane sizes, see page 15.)

Tools

Side-cutters
Small/medium bodkin or awl
Round-nosed pliers
Flexible steel tape measure

Instructions

No. 1: *Pierce* six of the base sticks and thread the other six through. *Tie in the slath* with two rounds of *pairing*, using the black 2.5 mm (No. 5) cane, treating each bunch of sticks as a single stick. On the third round, cut off the left-hand black weaver and replace it with a natural one. Pair around, dividing the sticks into pairs, and work nine rows without dividing the sticks further.

Cut a point on one end of each of the sticks 11.5 cm (4½ in) long and insert them into the weaving as far as they will comfortably go, one either side of each pair of sticks. Work a further six rows of pairing, still without separating the sticks, so that you have fifteen rows altogether.

On the next row, separate the sticks into pairs, which will alter the pattern. Cut a point on one end of the sticks 8 cm (3⅛ in) long and insert them in between each pair of sticks, pushing them in as far as they will comfortably go. Work eight more rows of pairing. Cut the ends of the weavers to rest at the back of the work, and cut all the sticks flush with the weaving. The mat should now measure 23.5 cm (9¼ in) across.

Cut a point on one end of each of the forty-eight border stakes and insert them one either side of each group of three sticks. Damp and *squeeze* the stakes and, with the top of the mat facing you, work a *four-rod behind two border*. Then work a *follow-on border*, threading each end underneath the one to its right and through to the other side of the work. *Trim* all the ends.

No. 2: *Pierce* five of the base sticks and thread the other five through. *Tie in the slath* with two rounds of *pairing*, using the natural 2.5 mm (No. 5) cane, treating each bunch of sticks as a single stick. On the third round, divide the bunches of sticks into a pair, a single and a pair, and work one more round without dividing the sticks further. On the fifth round, add a black weaver and work *three-rod waling*, dividing all the sticks into singles. Work five rows then cut the weavers, leaving the ends at the back. Put the weavers back into the same spaces that they finished in, in the same sequence, but this time work the wale from right to left. Complete another five rows and cut the weavers, leaving the ends at the back.

Changing the direction of the wale

Cut a point on one end of the sticks 11 cm (4⅜ in) long and insert them to the right of each stick as far as they will comfortably go. Put the weavers back into the spaces where the ends were left, in the same sequence, and this time work a three-rod wale from left to right. Do six rows, cut the weavers, work another four rows from right to left and again cut the weavers. The mat should now measure 22.5 cm (8⅞ in).

Cut a point on one end of each of the forty border stakes and insert them one either side of each pair of sticks. Take three black 2.5 mm (No. 5) weavers and work a single round of three-rod wale, separating the border stakes as much as possible. Then damp the border stakes, *squeeze* them, and work a *trac border*, going behind one stake, in front of the next and behind the next, leaving the ends at the back. *Trim* all the ends.

No. 3: *Pierce* six of the base sticks and thread the other six through. Using black 2.5 mm (No. 5) cane, *tie in the slath* with two rows of *pairing*, treating the bunches of sticks as a single stick. Do another row of pairing, separating the sticks into pairs. On the fourth row, add two natural 2.5 mm (No. 5) weavers in the two spaces immediately to the right of the black weavers. Continue pairing for fourteen rows, chasing the two colours and keeping the natural ahead all the time. Leave the weavers.

Adding the natural weavers on the fourth row

Cut a point on one end of each of the sticks 11 cm (4⅜ in) long and insert them one either side of each pair of sticks. Continue pairing, separating the sticks into pairs, for twenty-four rows in total. Cut the natural pair of weavers and work one more row with the black pair.

Cut a point on one end of each of the fifty-two border stakes and insert forty-eight of them one either side of the pairs of sticks. Put in the four spare stakes and work a *rope border*, taking each bunch of stakes over one to the right and back to the other side. *Trim* all the ends.

No. 4: *Pierce* six of the base sticks and thread the other six through. With a length of 2 mm (No. 3) cane, *tie in the slath* with two rounds of *pairing*, treating the bunches of sticks as a single stick. On the third round, separate the sticks into pairs and work a further four rounds. Cut the weavers at the back. Take one black and two natural 2.5 mm (No. 5) weavers and work six rounds of *three-rod waling* on the pairs of sticks. On the seventh row, cut the black and one of the natural weavers and swap them over. Work five more rows, making a total of twelve rows of waling.

Swapping the weavers to change the pattern

Cut a point on one end of each of the sticks 10 cm (4 in) long and insert them one either side of the pairs of sticks. Continue waling for six rows, separating the groups of sticks into pairs. The mat should now measure 23.5 cm (9¼ in).

Cut a point on one end of each of the forty-eight border stakes and insert them one either side of the pairs of sticks. Damp and *squeeze* them and, with the wrong side of the mat towards you, work a *four-rod behind two border*. *Trim* all the ends.

Right: *Cane shoulder bag*

Cane Shoulder Bag

The shape of this bag, I was told by a Japanese lady, is very similar to a traditional Japanese fish basket! I was not aware of that when I designed it, but looking at it now, I think I must have had some sense of its Japanese shape because of my choice of cord and tassels, which give it an oriental look. You could easily make this basket into a secure handbag by adding a leather lining and a zipped opening.

Finished measurements

Height: 21.5 cm (8½ in)
Maximum width: 16.5 cm (6½ in)
Width at opening: 11 cm (4⅜ in)
Maximum length: 27.5 cm (10¾ in)
Length of opening: 20 cm (8 in)

Materials

200 g (7¼ oz) centre cane:
    75 g (2½ oz) of 3 mm (No. 8) natural – 4 stakes
      98 cm (38½ in) long, 16 stakes 86 cm (33¾ in)
      long, and 8 stakes 40 cm (15¾ in) long
    25 g (1 oz) each of 2.5 mm (No. 5) in jade green,
      black and orange
    50 g (1¾ oz) of 2 mm (No. 3) natural
2 metal D–rings 2 cm (¾ in) wide
1 m (1 yd) of cord for handle
2 large beads, with holes large enough to take the
    cord doubled – mine are pieces of bamboo with
    drilled 8 mm (⁵⁄₁₆ in) holes

(NOTE: For American equivalents of cane sizes, see page 15.)

Tools

Flexible steel tape measure
Side-cutters
Small/medium bodkin or awl
Round-nosed pliers

Instructions

Pierce the sixteen stakes in the centre and thread them onto the four long ones in pairs. With a length of 2 mm (No. 3) natural, start *pairing* by looping the cane around four stakes at one end of the slath, and work along to the other end. Take another length of the same cane, loop it around the four stakes at this end, and *reverse pair* back to the start. Work one complete round of each, then work another one and a half rounds of each, at the same time dividing the stakes at each end into pairs, so that you have five rows altogether. This is called *chain pairing*.

Cut a point on one end of each of the remaining eight stakes and insert them in pairs between the divided end stakes. Using one length of the same cane, start *packing* on blocks of four pairs of stakes, beginning with a group of four at one end, so that the blocks are regularly spaced with one at each end and two along each side. Take one length each of orange, jade and black cane and insert them in that order into the three spaces created by the four pairs of stakes at one end.

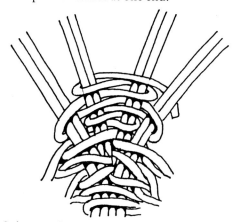

Stakes inserted and first set of packing completed at one end of the base

Work a *three-rod wale* along to the other end. Add another three weavers (same colour, same order) in the three spaces at this end, and then *reverse wale* with those to the other side. Work both sets of weavers back to the ends where they started and, leaving a set of weavers at each end, start packing again using the 2 mm (No. 3) natural. Centre the blocks of packing in the dips created by the previous blocks. Keep the work tight and well pushed down. Continue working one complete round of each row of waling and then packing in the dips.

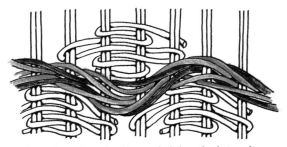

Start of second set of packing worked above the chain waling

This basket needs careful *shaping*: curve the ends upwards on the third packing row but keep the sides curving outwards until the fourth packing row when you should start to turn them upwards. From then on, curve the work gently inwards, checking the measurements as you go. If the opening at the top gets too small, the basket will not be very useful.

After the fourteenth packing row, work the two rows of waling and then put the D-rings over two stakes at the centre of each end. Cut the stake on the left of the left-hand pair and the right stake of the right-hand pair, then cut the right-hand stake of all the other pairs level with the top of the work, which should have a wavy edge. Damp the remaining stakes, *squeeze*, and work a *three-rod border*. *Trim* all the ends and *singe* any hairs.

D-rings in place

The handle is attached by taking the cord and threading it through the bead and the D-ring, then back up through the bead again. Tie a knot at the end of the cord and fluff out the ends.

Attaching the handle

Note: This basket could be made bigger by scaling up the materials but if you want to enlarge it by adding extra stakes, remember that you must use a number of stakes that divides by three for the waling pattern to work, and by six for the packing blocks to come in the right place (the result of the latter calculation will determine the number of stakes over which the blocks of packing should be worked). Don't forget also to add extra length to the stakes if you decide to make the basket bigger.

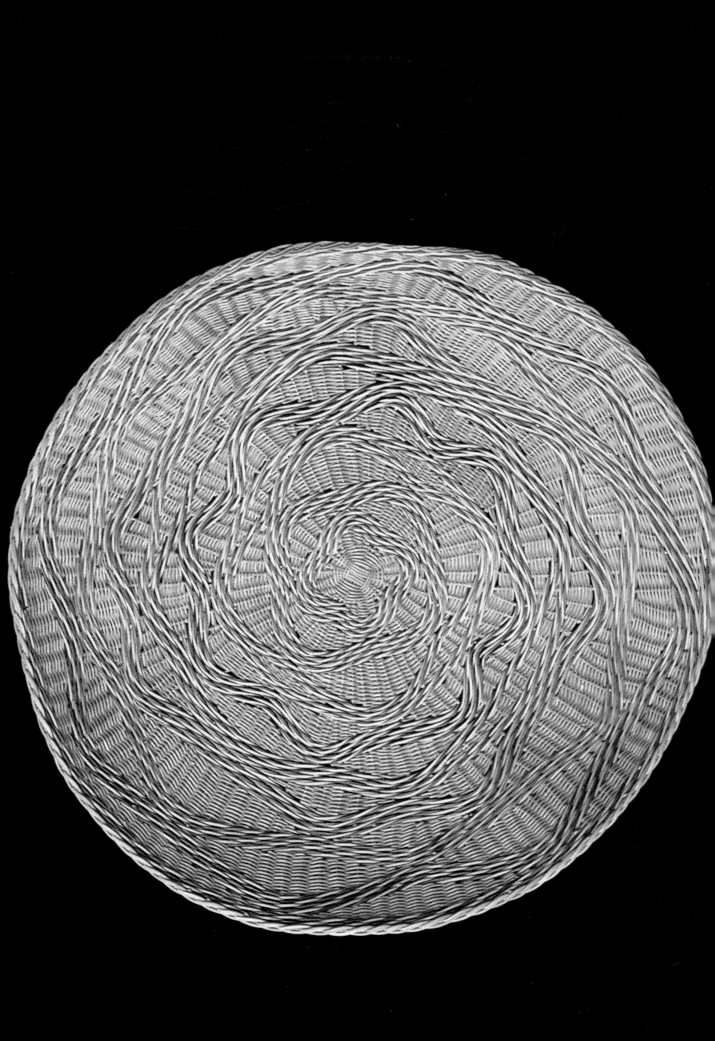

Orange Cane Platter

I like to make my platters big in order to show off the patterns, but you can of course make yours smaller than the one here just by shortening the length of your original stakes and scaling down the size of the material.

Finished measurements

Depth: 13 cm (5⅛ in)
Width: 70 cm (27½ in)

Materials

575 g (20 oz) dyed cane:
    250 g (9 oz) of 3 mm (No. 8) orange – 12 stakes
        100 cm (39½ in) long, 9 stakes 50 cm (19¾ in)
        long, and 8 stakes 45 cm (17¾ in) long
    175 g (6 oz) of 2 mm (No. 3) orange
    75 g (2½ oz) of 2 mm (No. 3) yellow
    75 g (2½ oz) of 2 mm (No. 3) dark green

(NOTE: For American equivalents of cane sizes, see page 15.)

Tools

Flexible steel tape measure
Side-cutters
Small/medium bodkin or awl
Round-nosed pliers

Instructions

Pierce six of the 100 cm (39½ in) long stakes and thread the other six through. *Tie in the slath* with two rounds of *pairing*, using the 2 mm (No. 3) orange and treating each bunch of stakes as a single stick. Then do two more rounds, dividing the stakes into groups of three. On the fifth round, divide all the stakes into singles. Now start *packing* in four blocks of five stakes, leaving one stake empty between blocks (you should have twenty-four stakes). Begin the packing at the centre of the blocks of five stakes, work out and then back in again. Push the work up tight.

Add the nine stakes 50 cm (19¾ in) long by cutting a point on one end of each and pushing them into the packing beside another stake. Look for the places where the gaps between the stakes are biggest. Put two stakes into three blocks of packing and three into the fourth. This brings the number of stakes up to thirty-three (it is essential for this pattern to work to have a number of stakes that is divisible by four, plus one extra).

Left: *Orange cane platter*

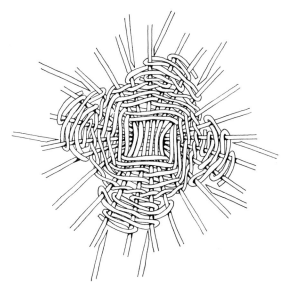

Inserting nine stakes into the blocks of packing

Now start the *waling*. Put four single weavers into four consecutive spaces in the order yellow, green, yellow, green, and work four rounds of waling – but not the usual four-rod. This wale goes over two stakes and under two stakes, thus creating a spiral effect. Separate the new stakes as you come to them.

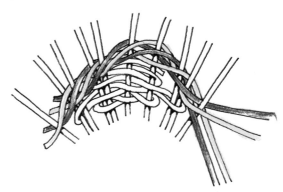

Positioning of the weavers to create the spiral pattern

At the end of these four rows, take the weaves onto the top of the next block of packing and then leave them. Do not cut them. Using the 2 mm (No. 3) orange again, pack on three blocks of eight stakes and one block of nine, in the dips created by the first lot of packing. Start in the middle as before, work out and then back in again, but this time there are no empty stakes.

Add the eight stakes 45 cm (17¾ in) long, pushing them into the packing, again where the gaps between the stakes are biggest. Try to distribute them as evenly as possible around the work. You will now have forty-one stakes. Pick up the yellow and green weavers once more and work another four rounds of waling. Keep the work

105

tight, but always follow the curves of the packing; there should be no gaps between the packing and the waling blocks. As before, finish at the top of one of the blocks of packing. Pack in the dips again with the orange cane, this time working over three blocks of ten stakes and one of eleven.

From here on you simply continue in the same manner, packing in the dips and following around with waling. When the blocks of packing get too big, make more smaller ones. When the gaps between the stakes become too large for neatness, add more stakes – but always in multiples of four to maintain the waling pattern. Any new stakes should be added immediately after a round of packing and separated with the waling. This makes the additions less obvious than they would be if this were done the other way around. At this stage the outline will be wavy but the weaving should be quite flat, like a mat.

When the work is about 40 cm (15¾ in) across, start the *shaping* by gently pulling the waling tighter as you go. The angle of the stakes will be a guide as to how much of a curve you are creating. Continue in this manner until the work measures 67 cm (26½ in) across at the widest point.

The work now has to be brought back to a circular shape for the border. This is done by taking a piece of the 3 mm (No. 8) cane and with a dressmaking pin fixing it about 1 cm (⅜ in) from its end to the centre of the basket. Adjust the cane to fit the shape of the basket and cut it level with the highest point of the weaving. Swing it round, marking each stake level with the end of it. Check each time that the measure sits right on the surface of the basket. Using a combination of packing and *rapping* the work up tight where necessary, you should be able to fill the gaps up to the marks by means of the *filling-in packing* technique.

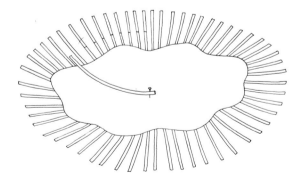

The method of marking the stakes to form a circle

When you are happy with the shape, add another two rows of waling. To put the border on, wet the stakes and *squeeze* them, then work a *three-rod border* from the underside, so that the cut ends are underneath the basket.

106

Willow and Tape Striped Basket

This is a strong all-purpose basket, which can be worked with stripes of any width and with as many colours as you want. The colours and pattern for this basket were inspired by a helter-skelter that I photographed at a south coast funfair on one of those crisp but very bright winter days.

Finished measurements

Height to border: 42 cm (16½ in)
Width at border: 54 cm (21¼ in)
Width of base: 38 cm (15 in)

Materials

10 willow base sticks 40 cm (15¾ in) long and approximately 8 mm (⁵⁄₁₆ in) wide
Approximately 36 4 ft (1.20 m) rods for weaving the base
40 medium-thick 6 ft (1.80 m) rods for stakes
8 thin 6 ft (1.80 m) rods for upsetting
68 m (74 yd) of 1 cm (⅜ in) wide polypropylene tape or flat-band cane – 34 m (37 yd) of each of two colours. If the tape or cane is narrower, allow extra length
Approximately 30 m (33 yd) of 3.75 mm (No. 12) cane dyed cerise
2 pieces 58 cm (22¾ in) long of 8 mm (⁵⁄₁₆ in) handle cane
4 2.5 cm (1 in) carpet tacks

(NOTE: For American equivalents of cane sizes, see page 15.)

Tools

Secateurs
Medium/large bodkin or awl
Knife
Scissors
Side-cutters
Flexible steel tape measure

Instructions

Pierce five of the willow base sticks in the centre and thread the other five through. Weave a *round base*, using the 4 ft (1.20 m) rods, finishing on tips when the base measures 36 cm (14 in). Trim off the base sticks and *stake-up* with the forty medium-thick 6 ft (1.80 m) rods. Work one round

Right: *Willow and tape striped basket*

of *four-rod waling*, using the eight thin 6 ft (1.80 m) rods, starting the two sets by their butts on opposite sides of the base.

Cut the tape or flat-band cane into forty 1.5 m (1⅔ yd) lengths (do not forget to allow more material if it is narrower than 1 cm/⅜ in), consisting of twenty lengths in each colour. Lay in the tape in blocks of four, weaving the ends in on themselves. After each block, work a row of *pairing*, starting it by looping the cane around the stake. The next piece of tape is put in around the same stake on which the pairing began.

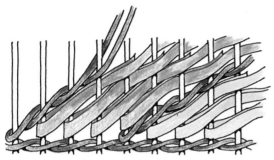

The tape laid in in blocks of four

Continue *French randing* in this manner until the work measures 37 cm (14½ in) high. Thread the ends of the tape back on themselves as before. Leave the ends of the cane where they finished. Using another two pieces of cane, work two rows of pairing. Check that the basket is level at the top and then work a *three-rod behind two border*. Pick up the ends of the cane from the side weaving and tuck them into the cane pairing under the border. *Trim* carefully.

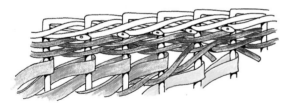

Tucking the ends into the top pairing

Soak the handle cane, cut *slypes* on each end, and insert the bows on opposite sides of the basket. Make each handle about 16 cm (6¼ in) wide and 6 cm (2½ in) high. Insert two pieces of tape (one of each colour) approximately 80 cm (31½ in) long down beside the handle bow and twist them around the bow together (to create a striped effect). Tuck the ends down beside the other end of the handle bow.

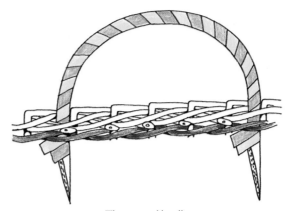

The wrapped handle

Working on the outside of the basket, thread a length of cane under the border to the left of the left-hand end of the handle, leaving about 15 cm (6 in) of cane at the back. Wrap the cane loosely around the handle so that it crosses the front of it three times, then bring it to the front at the right of the handle and thread it through from the outside to the inside under the border. Take the cane back over the handle in the spaces left by the first crossing and again through under the border from the outside, to the left of the handle bow. Work the cane back across to the other side once again and leave it there. The strands should be evenly spaced so that you can see the stripes underneath. Finish by threading the ends away into the pairing as inconspicuously as possible. *Trim* the ends and *tack the handles*.

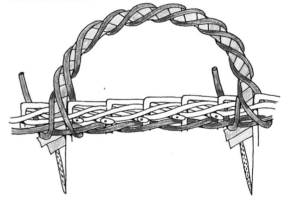

Roping the handle with cane

Handles such as these are strong and attractive (see photograph on page 82) but if you intend to carry your basket often heavily loaded, it would probably be more comfortable to hold if you *wrap* or *rope* the handles without any gaps.

Right: *Willow and card round linen basket*

Willow and Card
Round Linen Basket

This is not a difficult basket to make if you have used willow before. It also offers a good opportunity to use a colour scheme that will co-ordinate with the colours of the room in which the basket will be kept. You can even use left-over wall emulsion to decorate the card.

Finished measurements

Height to top of lid (excluding handle): 62 cm (24½ in)
Width at border: 36 cm (14 in)

Materials

7 base sticks 30 cm (12 in) long cut from butts of 6 ft (1.80 m) white willow
7 sticks 38 cm (15 in) long cut from butts of 6 ft (1.80 m) white willow for the lid
28 6 ft (1.80 m) well-matched willow rods for stakes
8 thick 4 ft (1.20 m) willow rods for the upsett
Approximately 60 4 ft (1.20 m) willow rods for weaving
4 strips of painted cardboard 13 cm (5⅛ in) wide and 115 cm (45¼ in) long
1 piece of painted card 36 cm (14 in) square
Approximately 35 m (38 yd) of 3.5 mm (No. 11) cane dyed to complement the painted card
Piece of handle cane 125 cm (49¼ in) long, natural

(NOTE: For American equivalents of cane sizes, see page 15.)

Tools

Secateurs
Medium bodkin or awl
Knife
Side-cutters
Round-nosed pliers
Hot-glue gun (or quick-drying glue suitable for cardboard)
Heavy-duty scissors
Flexible steel tape measure

Instructions

Pierce four of the base sticks and thread the other three through. Using the 4 ft (1.20 m) rods, weave a *round base*, finishing on tips when it measures 26 cm (10¼ in) across. Trim off the base sticks and *stake-up* with the twenty-eight 6 ft (1.80 m) rods. Work a single row of *four-rod upsett*, using the eight stout 4 ft (1.20 m) rods and starting one set each side of the base.

With 4 ft (1.20 m) rods, *fitch* at two or three intervals up the basket, making sure that the shape is quite cylindrical. This fitching will be cut off later so it does not need to be beautiful – its purpose is to control the shape. Mark the stakes at a height of 58 cm (22¾ in) and at that point work one row of neat fitching; this row will stay in. Start with two tips (not too thin, about 3 mm/ ⅛ in) and work these two thirds of the way round the basket. Then join in two equal-sized rods using butts. Work the tips until they overlap the beginning so that there is an equal depth of willow all the way round. Check that the top edge of the fitching is level and consistently the same height

110

from the ground. Resoak the stakes if necessary and work a *four-rod behind two border*. Trim all the stakes and keep the tips to use on the lid.

With the basket upside down, work a *three-rod wale* in cane on top of the border. Turn the basket back up the right way and work a three-rod wale on top of the upsett. Now *rand* a strip of card in on top of this wale. Overlap the ends and fasten with hot glue. Then work a second row of three-rod wale in cane over the top of the card and add another strip of card, making sure you weave over and under the same stakes as previously. Cut out the willow fitching as you reach it.

Continue in this manner until all four strips are in place and each strip is separated by a wale. If on the last row you find that you have not got enough room for the card, you can trim it to fit. If, on the other hand, you are left with a gap, you can either add another wale at the top or push every-thing up and add another one at the bottom. If that is still not enough, do both. If, however, there is not enough space for a wale, just rand a single cane between the card and the existing wale.

Decorate the basket by inserting cane to the left of a stake at the upsett on the outside. Push it down so that it is firmly held, then thread it through the wales diagonally from one to the next. When you reach the border, thread the canes up through the wale and as far into the border as possible. It may be possible to thread them right through to the left of the stake and if so, *trim* them flush with the border afterwards.

Making the lid: Pierce four of the 38 cm (15 in) long sticks and thread the other three through. *Tie in the slath*, using willow, with three rows of pairing, treating each bunch of sticks as one stick. On the fourth row, separate all the sticks and leave the ends at the back. Work a single row of three-rod wale using cane.

To cut the card for the lid, which has to be done in two sections, position the slath on the card so that the edge of the woven area aligns with the edge of the card. Draw around the slath and then draw a semi-circle between the ends of the sticks so that the card will come to within 3.5–4 cm (1⅜–1½ in) of the outside edge of the finished lid. Cut the card along both these lines and use this piece as the template for the other half. The two pieces of card should each be bigger than a semi-circle so that they will overlap when they are in position. Weave the pieces into place by pushing them between the sticks, making sure that you go over and under alternate sticks. Trim and glue the overlapping card.

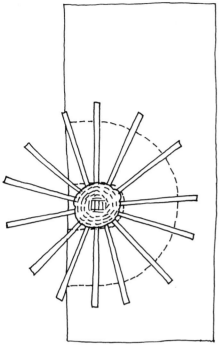

Cutting the card for the lid

For the border stakes, use fourteen of the tips that were cut off the main stakes. Cut *slypes* on them and, using a bodkin to work a space, push them into the centre slath to the right of the sticks on both sides of the card. Make sure that they are held firmly. Work a single row of three-rod waling with cane, separating all the sticks and stakes. Then work a three-rod wale with the tips of 4 ft (1.20 m) rods until the lid is within 7 mm (¼ in) of its final size.

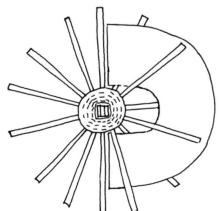

Inserting the card between the stakes

Take the remaining tips from the main stakes and insert them into the waling to the left of the sticks. If necessary cut their butt ends slightly so that they are the same width as the stakes already inserted. Trim any stick ends which extend beyond the weaving. With the underside of the lid facing you, work a *three-rod border*, then trim the stakes. *Make a rim* with handle cane or willow and lace it to the underside of the lid.

Making the handle: Make a bow out of handle cane and slype the ends of it on the inside. Thread them through the lid just inside the willow centre and adjust to the required height. *Squeeze* each end of handle cane so that it folds flat up against the underside of the lid. Then take a length of cane and tuck it into the slath on the underside, threading it through the lid so that it comes out beside one end of the handle bow. Wind it round the bow three times, take it through the lid, and then bring it back up the same end of the handle, catching one of the folded ends of the bow underneath. Wind the cane back to the other side, then take it down through the lid. Catching the other end of the bow, thread the end into the underside of the slath.

Decorate the top of the lid in the same manner as the main basket. Lastly, *varnish* the basket thoroughly inside and out.

Willow and Cane Shopping Basket

This is a classic shopping basket, not so essential now that we shop by the trolley load, and unfortunately its open shape is an invitation to purse snatchers in town . . . but it is ideal for the fruit and veg street market, to collect flowers with, to keep the knitting in, or to carry books in.

Finished measurements

Height to border: 21 cm (8¼ in)
Height including handle: 33 cm (13 in)
Length at border: 49 cm (19½ in)
Length at base: 32 cm (12½ in)
Width at border: 31 cm (12¼ in)
Width at base: 21 cm (8¼ in)

Materials

3 willow base sticks 34 cm (13½ in) long and approximately 6 mm (¼ in) wide
7 willow base sticks 22 cm (8¾ in) long and approximately 6 mm (¼ in) wide
Approximately 28 medium-thick 4 ft (1.20 m) rods for weaving the base
34 thick 4 ft (1.20 m) or fine 5 ft (1.5 m) rods for stakes
16 thick 4 ft (1.20 m) rods for upsetting and the top wale
15 m (16½ yd) of 1 cm (⅜ in) wide flat-band cane or polypropylene tape dyed turquoise
13 m (14¼ yd) of 5 mm (³⁄₁₆ in) lapping or flat-band cane dyed cerise
8.5 m (9¼ yd) of 2.6 mm (No. 6) cane dyed yellow
8.5 m (9¼ yd) of 2.6 mm (No. 6) cane dyed royal blue
2 90 cm (36 in) lengths of willow cut from butts of 6 ft (1.80 m) rods for the handle bows
1 cm (⅜ in) tacks for the handle

(NOTE: For American equivalents of cane sizes, see page 15.)

Tools

Secateurs
Medium/large bodkin or awl
Knife
Scissors
Side-cutters
Flexible steel tape measure

Instructions

Pierce the seven short prepared base sticks and thread the three long sticks through. Spread the short sticks out evenly, keeping a pair together at each end of the slath. There should be 16 cm (6¼ in) from the outside of one pair to the outside of the pair at the other end.

Weave the base, using two sets of rods, *randing* them along the sides and *pairing* around the ends. Finish on tips when the base measures 18 cm (7 in) wide and 30 cm (12 in) long. *Rap* if necessary to get a regular shape.

Trim off the base sticks and then *stake-up*, putting two stakes to each of the sticks around the

Left: Willow and cane shopping basket

ends of the base and single stakes to the three sticks on each side. Put these singles in so that they will be to the right of the base sticks when they are *pricked up* (looking from the outside of the basket). This will ensure that the spaces for the handles will be centrally positioned on each side. *Upsett*, using two sets of four rods inserted by the butts at opposite ends of the basket. Work one row of *four-rod waling*, then *drop a rod* and continue with three rods, allowing the stakes to flow out a little. Work four rows or 3.5 cm (1⅜ in) of waling.

Starting with a wide strip, rand using wide and narrow cane in alternating rows. Concentrate on the shape; you need to make the basket flow out more at the ends than the sides. Work twenty rows, finishing with a narrow band.

In order to level up the work you must work one *packing* row at each end. Using the wide cane, weave it over fourteen stakes centrally at each end but cut a taper on the end of the strip so that it blends into the top edge of the weaving. The end is taken round the last stake and woven back along the row beneath it until it is held securely.

Using the 4 ft (1.20 m) rods, work three rows of *waling*, starting and finishing on tips. Check that the work is level and rap if necessary. Work a *three-rod border* and *trim*. Cut long *slypes* on the two soaked handle bows and insert them beside the central stake on each side of the basket, alternating butt ends. The top of the bow should be 32 cm (12½ in) from the base inside the basket.

Now decorate the sides, using the 2.6 mm (No. 6) cane. Work one row threading it under the narrow bands of cane from top to bottom and the next row in the other colour from bottom to top. This creates a pattern like *chain pairing*. The ends of each piece are overlapped under the bands, but it is important to make these joins along the sides of the basket where the weaving will be tighter and will hold the ends in place better.

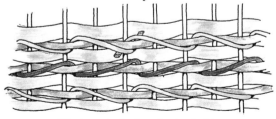

The decoration in place, showing the join

Wrap the handle with a 3 m (3¼ yd) length of the turquoise, using three 2.6 mm (No. 6) canes as the leader pattern, working two wraps under the three canes and one over. Then wind a length of the cerise around the handle, tucking it under the three canes – use a bodkin to ease the way for this. Secure each end of the handle bow with a tack.

It is a good idea to *varnish* the cane on this basket, but it is not necessary to varnish the willow.

PLAITING METHOD

This technique is used on baskets from all over the world and dates back to the beginnings of the craft. It is used mainly in those areas where the indigenous materials come in the form of (or can be made into) long, flat, flexible strips, such as reeds, bamboo, canes, split timber, bark, and so on.

The essence of the technique is that all the elements are of similar width and thickness, and that the same elements which are woven to form the base also form the sides. One of the characteristics of a plaited basket is that although the base may be square or rectangular, the top will automatically form into a round or oval shape. There is no distinction between stakes and weavers, unlike the stake and strand method where bases are often made separately and staked-up with new elements. Depending on the materials used, the results can be either rigid containers or soft bags. In Scandinavia, for example, strips of pine are used to make strong square shopping baskets, whereas in New Zealand the Maoris use flax to make soft, flexible bags.

Right: *Selection of baskets made by the plaiting method*

Materials

Any material that is flexible and in the form of long strips, either naturally or by having been cut, is suitable for plaiting. Some can be bought from a basketry materials supplier, such as flat-band or lapping canes and rushes; you might already have others in your garden, such as iris or flax; and some materials you might find, buy, or otherwise acquire, such as plastic packaging tapes, cardboard, old film, heavy-duty polythene, vinyl flooring, leather, fabric tape, wood veneer (tricky but rewarding), and so on. The guiding principle for my choice of materials is whether the time and effort required to prepare them is going to be justified by the end product. Hand-knitting long strips out of unpicked jumpers and using them to weave with may be cheap, but will the resulting basket be worth having?

My favourite material for plaiting with is corrugated cardboard, for lots of reasons. It makes a fairly rigid basket; it is strong; it can be

painted; and it is easy to cut up. It also has one other big advantage: it is free – tons of it are thrown away daily in our towns and cities.

When I first tried using cardboard, I had been making coloured baskets, using dyed cane, for a while and I was beginning to feel limited by only being able to create woven patterns. I used to paint before I started basket making and I missed the directness of application of colour that painting offers. Cardboard provides a perfect surface for painting and I realized the potential of using painted cardboard in my baskets.

I first used cardboard strips in the stake and strand method, weaving them on cane stakes. I then tried plaiting them and this worked so well that I have been using cardboard ever since. My initial doubts about it being strong enough to take any weight were unfounded. After all, each basket is made with a double layer of cardboard throughout – and think how strong one cardboard box is. At first I also worried about the problem of getting caught in a shower of rain whilst carrying a cardboard bag, but several coats of varnish take care of that.

Left: *Plaiting materials*

Tools and Equipment

The tools and equipment needed for plaiting techniques are simple. You could probably do most things using just a knife and an awl or bodkin, but a few other items will make life easier. Different tools and pieces of equipment are required for different materials:

Cardboard
Heavy-duty scissors
Knife
Small- and medium-sized bodkin or awl
Large-eyed needle
1 m (1 yd) rigid steel rule
Clothes pegs (US: clothespins)
Hot-glue gun
Band saw with knife blade
Hole punch
Eyelet punch
Hammer
Stapler

Cane or other materials in strips
Heavy-duty scissors or secateurs
Knife
Small- or medium-sized bodkin or awl
Large-eyed needle
Flexible steel tape measure
Clothes pegs (US: clothespins)
Stapler

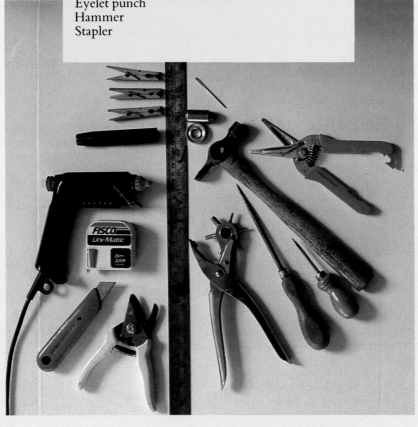

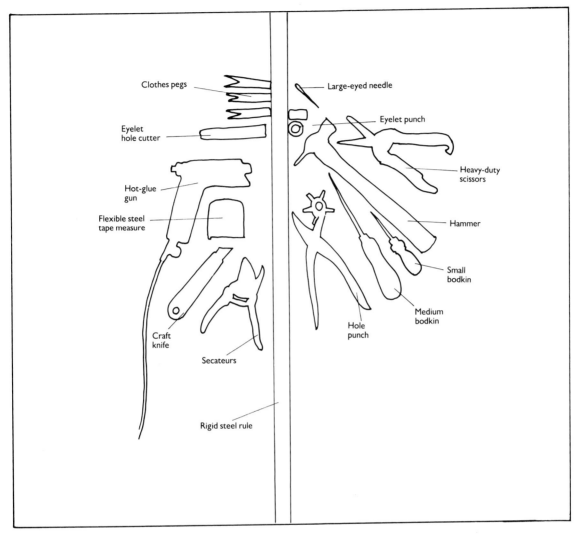

Clothes pegs

Eyelet
hole cutter

Hot-glue
gun

Flexible steel
tape measure

Craft
knife

Secateurs

Rigid steel rule

Large-eyed needle

Eyelet punch

Heavy-duty
scissors

Hammer

Small
bodkin

Medium
bodkin

Hole
punch

Heavy-duty scissors or secateurs: These should be capable of cutting cleanly through a double layer of cane.

Knives: These should have blades that can be replaced or sharpened effectively. Craft knives are ideal.

Bodkins or awls: These are the same as those used for the stake and strand method (see page 19).

Large-eyed needles: Darning or upholstery needles are suitable as long as they are able to take cotton cord or string.

Flexible steel tape measure: The retractable type, as described on page 19, is the most useful.

Rigid steel rule: This is essential when cutting cardboard strips by hand.

Clothes pegs (US: clothespins): These are used to hold the work in progress. At least twenty are needed for most jobs. Choose ones with a good grip.

Hot-glue gun: This is an electric, gun-shaped, glue dispenser. It heats the glue first, making it very quick-acting. It provides an effective way of joining cardboard strips.

Band saw with knife blade: This is an electric saw used mainly for woodwork. It can be small enough to fit on a bench top or free-standing, and it provides the quickest way to cut cardboard strips. A blade designed for use on wood will create burrs or furry edges on your strips, but a knife blade cuts cleanly. If you intend making a few cardboard baskets and you have access to a band saw, this blade is worth investing in.

Hole punch, eyelet punch and hammer: These items are used to insert eyelets for handles. In Britain yacht chandlers are the best source for them, whereas in America they can be obtained at craft stores.

Stapler: This can be useful for joining the ends of tape used for handles.

Left: Tools required for the plaiting method

Preparation of Materials for Use

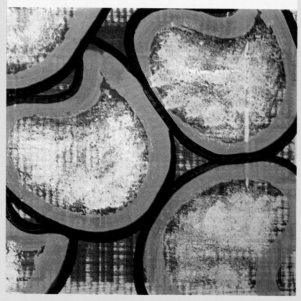

Cane

All you need to do to prepare cane is dye it if you want it coloured, cut it to length, and damp it. For instructions on how to carry out these processes, refer to the chapter on Preparation of Materials in the stake and strand section (see page 20).

Cardboard

Look for cardboard boxes made of card which is not too thick. Some cardboard has a double layer of corrugations and this is usually too heavy to work with, so avoid it if you can. (If you are desperate, though, it is possible to peel off the inner layer of corrugations.) Open the box out down the seam and cut off the flaps – it is the long strip down the middle that you want. Check that any corrugations run across the strip – sometimes boxes are put together so that the longest part runs along the corrugations and these are no good for our purposes.

Decorating the cardboard

You can use many media – paint, crayon, felt-tip pen, etc. – to decorate your cardboard. I use paint almost exclusively because it gives such strong colour, and I use a mixture of different types, mainly for economy. I buy white household emulsion in a matt or silk finish (US equivalent: flat latex) and mix it with PVA (plastic-based) primary colours to create all pastel shades. I also use the PVA primaries straight out of the bottle and mix them with each other. It is a good idea to have two of each – for example, two blues such as cobalt and ultramarine – because you can mix many more colours that way. Sometimes I choose acrylic paint if I want very intense colour for a special job, but I use this sparingly as it is expensive.

Whenever feasible you should decorate the cardboard on the printed side as this is usually slightly less impervious than the other side and will not therefore absorb as much paint. I like to use the printing on the box as part of the design so I do not usually cover it all up. However, if you want to make an all-over pale pink basket you would probably do better to paint the cardboard on the side without any printing.

Cutting strips

To cut the strips for plaiting you need a sharp knife and a rigid steel rule 1 m (1 yd) long. First cut one edge of the cardboard level, then measure off your strips from that edge. Alternatively, to save time, use a band saw if you have access to one.

Below: *Paints and decorated cardboard*

Weaves

There are as many different weaves in the plaiting method as there are in stake and strand basketry, including the aptly named 'mad' weave. However, I am going to deal with only two basic weaves – checkweave and twill weave – because by using different colours and surface embellishments infinite variations can be created with these.

Checkweave

This weave is the equivalent of randing in stake and strand basketry. A number of weavers or strips are laid down and an equal number are woven into them, over one and under one, at right angles. This order is alternated for each row. Checkweave can be worked into a tight fabric with no gaps between the strands, or as an open weave.

Checkweave base, using sixteen strips

This can be made in cane or with cardboard strips. Checkweave is difficult to work closely in cane because the material is fairly thick and rigid in relation to its width. Bear this in mind when designing your basket and use the inevitable gaps for threading other materials into.

An even number of weavers in each direction makes it easier to border the basket. An odd number causes the weave to spiral and, as a result, a border started at a certain height will end up a row higher or lower than at the beginning. You could, of course, use this as part of the design.

How it is done: If using **cane**, lay eight strips side by side on the work surface. Position them with equally sized gaps between them and tape across the ends to hold them down. Mark the middle two strips in their centres and weave the remaining strips across them in an over one under one pattern. Start in the centre and work an equal number of strips above and below the centre mark, so that the woven area is centrally situated.

When you have woven all the strips, put clothes pegs (US: clothespins) at the corners of the woven area to hold the work in place. You are then ready to make the corners, thus forming the base.

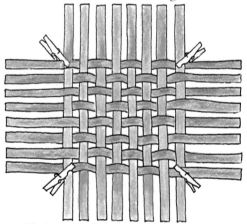

Checkweave worked in the open manner using cane

It is unlikely that you will break a cane weaver provided you keep the material damp while you work with it. If you do, however, simply overlap the ends by at least three strip widths and continue weaving as before. If the join is too bulky you can shave the material down a bit at that point.

If using **cardboard** checkweave needs to be done differently in order to make a solid fabric without gaps – the strength of a cardboard basket depends to a large extent on this.

Previous page: *Painted card wastepaper basket in checkweave; height c. 35 cm (13¾ in)*

Mark two strips in the centre and lay them across each other at right angles so that one mark is visible on each side. The point where the marks meet will be the centre of your finished woven area. Weave the other strips into place one at a time, making sure that you end up with an equal number of strips all the way round the centre mark.

Laying in the fifth weaver

It is important that the strips are woven as tightly as possible; trying to tighten the weaving at a later point tends to result in broken strips. To ensure that the weave is tight, fold the weavers that will be positioned over the new strips back on themselves, so that each new strip will butt up as closely as possible to the previous one. As you lay the folded strips back down over the new one, lift them up slightly first so that the new strip is not forced away, so creating a gap.

When all the strips have been woven, check that the weaving is square and, if necessary, tighten up any loose areas by pulling gently but firmly on the strips, being very careful not to break them. Peg the corners of the woven area to hold the work in place.

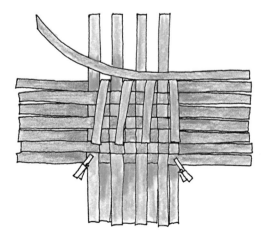

Laying in the last weaver

If a cardboard strip breaks while you are working (they do tend to until you learn to judge their strength), lay the two pieces on top of each other, squashing them first so that the double layer is not too bulky and making sure that they overlap by at least two strip widths. Continue weaving. Any ends left sticking out can be trimmed later.

Alternatively, you can glue the two pieces together using a hot-glue gun. Peel about 5 cm (2 in) of the corrugations off the back of one of the strips and cut it off. Glue the remaining thin flap onto the other piece, making sure there is no gap between the pieces on the underside.

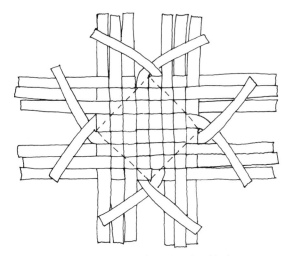

Position of the corners for a square-based basket

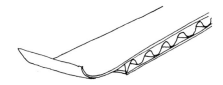

Cardboard strip with a portion of the corrugations removed

Position of the corners for an oblong-based basket

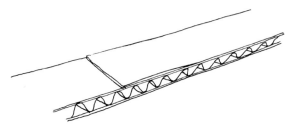

Finished glued join

Forming the base: Unlike stake and strand basketry, when using plaiting techniques the woven area from which the base will be formed is always square, regardless of the final shape of the basket. To define the base area and in order to work the sides of the basket, corners have to be made. It is the positioning of these on the square woven area that determines the shape of the basket.

Making corners: First decide what shape the base of your basket is to be. For a square basket the corners are made at the centres of the sides. For a rectangular basket they are made near two diagonally opposite corners of the woven area. For an envelope shape they are made at two of the original corners of the woven area. These all produce regular shapes but you could make the corners almost anywhere if you want to make asymmetrical shapes.

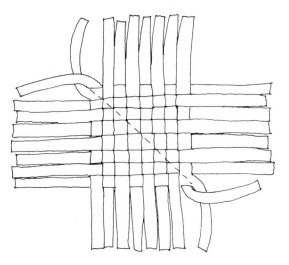

Position of the corners for an envelope-shaped basket

Left: *The two central weavers crossed over*

Below left: *Working the first weaver from the right*

Having decided on the shape, mark the point where each corner is to be made on the undecorated side of the relevant strips. This is very useful should you lose track of what you are doing later on. With the undecorated side of the strips uppermost, take the two strips which are marked and cross them over each other, making sure that you maintain the over one under one weave. Pull the strips so that they cross each other at right angles and put a clothes peg at the point between them. Do the same at each corner. The weaving will lift off the work surface on either side of the corners but do not worry about this.

Pick up the weavers on either side of each corner and weave them individually over and under all the strips that are at right angles to it. When you reach the clothes pegs at the original corners of the woven area, put one on the top of the diamond-shaped area you have just woven and begin to work another corner.

When the four corners have been built the areas in between (the corners of the original square area) are woven. Always work the lowest unwoven ends first and remember that every strip pointing to the left is woven into every strip pointing to the right, and vice versa. Also remember to try to keep the weaving as tight as possible (unless you are working an open weave, in which case you should try to maintain equally spaced gaps). Continue weaving until you have reached the ends of your strips or the desired height of the basket, whichever comes first. Then tighten any parts if necessary and peg everything to hold it. You are now ready to work a border.

Above left: *Completed corner*

Left: *Weaving between the corners*

Twill Weave

This pattern creates an effect like parquet flooring. Each strip is woven over and under two or more strips, with the pattern shifting by one strip each time. Here I describe how to work the over two under two version.

If you were to weave a square area of twill weave and make corners in the same manner as for checkweave, you would find that it is impossible to work the twill pattern up the sides of the basket. Twill weave has to radiate from the centre of the base. Unlike checkweave, therefore, this means that you have to decide whether you want a square or rectangular base before you start weaving, and alter the pattern accordingly.

Square base, using sixteen strips of thin card or cane

It is a good idea when attempting this for the first time to work it in two colours as this will help you to see what you are doing. Use one colour for the vertical strips and the other for the horizontal ones.

How it is done: Take eight strips of one colour and mark the centres on them. Lay them down side by side and tape them at one end to hold them on the table while you work. Take one strip of the other colour, mark it in the centre, and weave it over two and under two from left to right just above the centre line and lining up the mark in the centre. Subsequent strips are added above this one and lined up level with it. Take the second strip under one, over two, under one, over one, under two, and over one. Take the third strip under two, over two, under two, and over two. Take the fourth strip over one, under two, over one, under one, over two, and under one.

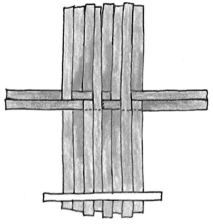

Laying in the second weaver

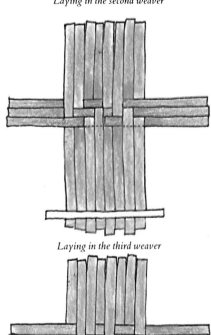

Laying in the third weaver

One half of the base completed

Laying in the first weaver

You should now see the pattern developing. If you look at what you have done you will notice that the woven area is divided down the middle and that there are no over twos or under twos crossing that line. The two sections are identical but in effect one of them has been rotated ninety degrees.

127

To weave the lower half of the square, follow the same instructions but work from right to left instead of left to right. Start at the centre and work outwards.

When you have finished you will find that there is a distinct division between the upper and lower sections and between left and right. You will end up with four identical quarters, each one at ninety degrees to its neighbour. The diagonally opposite quarters are mirror images of each other. It is worth spending some time coming to terms with the methods involved here before trying to make a basket.

Completed square base

If you are working with cane you will find that it is difficult to push the canes close together, so use a tool to help you. This can be either a piece of cane or willow sharpened to make a chisel-shaped end, or a screwdriver with a head about the same width as the cane which can be used to push the edge of the canes.

Rectangular base, using twenty strips of lightweight card or cane

This is made in the same way as the previous example, but with an extra section in the middle which means that only diagonally opposite quarters are identical.

How it is done: Lay out ten strips of one colour and mark the centres of the two middle ones. Work the first horizontal weaver from left to right under one, over two, under one, over one, under one, over two, and under two. This strip lies immediately above the centre line and subsequent ones are woven in above it. Take the second strip

Right: *Twill weave lidded box with two layers of painted card; height c. 25 cm (9¾ in)*

over two, under one, over one, under one, over two, under two, and over one. Take the third strip under two, over one, under one, over two, under two, and over two. Take the fourth strip

Laying in the first weaver

Laying in the second weaver

Laying in the third weaver

over one, under two, over two, under two, over two, and under one. Take the fifth strip over two, under one, over one, under two, over two, and under two.

Laying in the fourth weaver

One half of the base completed

The lower half of the weaving is worked similarly but from right to left. Note that there is an over one and under one at the four points where the corners will be. These are made in the usual manner and all weavers are then worked over or under two.

Completed rectangular base

You can of course work either of these bases with more strips as long as you use an even number in each direction. You can work out the corner positions on graph paper. If you are weaving with corrugated cardboard the same principle can be applied, but to make sure the weaving is tight it would be easier to work from the centre, having previously established a pattern on graph paper.

Borders

Borders in plaited work fall mainly into two groups: bound and woven. The type you choose will depend on the kind of material you are using and whether it will bend sharply back on itself without breaking, which it would need to do for a woven border.

Tightening the work

Initially, you will find that keeping the weaving tight as you work is very difficult. So, before you begin the border you should do any tightening that is necessary, because once the border has been started you cannot tighten up anything. It is worth spending time at this stage doing this because it will make a lot of difference to the durability and attractiveness of your basket.

How it is done: If using **cane**, pull on the individual canes to tighten them and use an implement, such as a bodkin, to help push the work up tight. If the loose area is well down in the work, use a bodkin to lift it and gradually work it up to the top edge.

If using **cardboard** you can pull on the card strips to a certain extent, but this does tend to snap them. Instead, lift up the loose strip with a bodkin into a loop and then work the loop one weave at a time back up to a point where you can pull the end of the strip without it breaking.

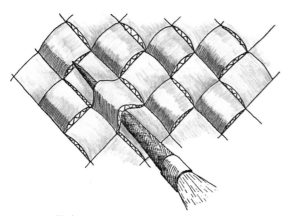

Tightening the weave when using cardboard

Whichever border you decide to use you must first mark the position of it on your basket. To do this, check that the work has been woven up to the same height all the way round and then determine the height at which the border is to be made. Count the rows of weaving up from one of the corners of the basket; in checkweave they will appear as diamonds and in twill weave they will be diagonal bars. Make a mark on the diamond or bar at the point where you require your border and then work round the basket marking the adjacent diamonds or bars. If you have marked them correctly you will find that all the ends of the marked strips will be pointing in the same direction. At this stage you need to decide which type of border to work.

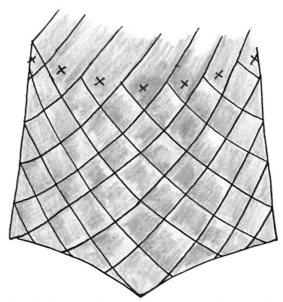

Counting the rows up from a corner in checkweave (five diamonds)

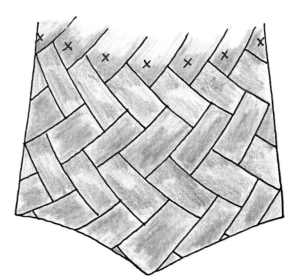

Counting the rows up from a corner in twill weave (five diagonal bars)

132

Bound Borders

These are made by stitching round the top of the basket to hold the work together, trimming the weavers, and then encasing the cut ends with two strips. These can be of the same material that you used for the weaving or something else. The strips are then held in place with stitching. You can vary the appearance of bound borders in many ways: by choice of binding material; by type of stitching; by how close together the stitching is; and by the material with which you stitch.

How it is done: If using **cane**, mark the border level all the way round as described opposite. Damp the cane and with a fine needle and strong linen thread, tack along the marked line. Alternatively, staple along it.

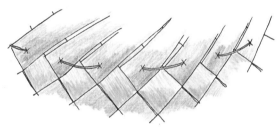

Tacking around the marked border line

With side-cutters or secateurs, cut off all the ends of the weavers in a straight line, immediately above the stitching or stapling. Then stitch two pieces of cane tightly in place, one inside and one outside and slightly staggered, so that they hide all the ends. Keep the stitching tight because the cane will shrink a bit as it dries. Overlap the ends when you get back to the start.

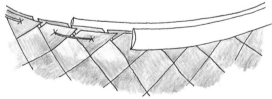

Staggering the start for a bound border

If using **cardboard**, work in exactly the same manner but stitch the cardboard as it is usually too thick to staple satisfactorily. Use a cotton or other strong cord, not too fine or it will tend to cut into the card. Make holes in the card for the needle to go through with a small bodkin. Tack round once and then tack again filling in the spaces left by the first round. Lay one strip of card (or other binding material) round the inside of the basket and another round the outside, staggering the ends. Stitch in place in the same manner as for cane. Overlap the ends when you get back to the start.

Stitching

The material you use for stitching can be anything that is strong, not stretchy, and not too thin otherwise it will tend to cut into the material when pulled tight. Some of the materials I use are polypropylene cords, cotton cords, plastic cane, chair cane, centre cane, split polypropylene tape and plastic thonging.

Like handles and fastenings, a bound border provides an opportunity for you to be inventive; but be careful not to get so carried away that the border becomes visually more important than the rest of the piece. It should complement the basket and for this reason your choice of colour and texture for the stitching material needs to be considered as well as the type and size of the stitching itself.

The amount of stitching material required will depend on how deep the border is and how far apart the stitches are to be. It is always more than you think and is certainly a minimum of four times the circumference of the basket. So make sure you have plenty of spare stitching cord before you start, in case it has to be joined.

The ends of the stitching are knotted together and any remaining ends can be threaded up into the border so that the knot sits tightly up against the binding on the inside.

The stitches can be as widely spaced as you like, but the weave can provide you with ready-made, evenly spaced holes, where the weavers cross each other. If these are too far apart then pierce the weave in between these holes and use those as well. The following are some of the most common stitches:

Overstitch: This is a very simple stitch. Take a length of stitching material and thread it through from the inside to the outside, leaving an end long enough to knot at the back. Take the thread over the top of the binding, down inside, then bring it through to the outside again, under the binding. Continue like this.

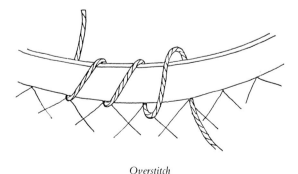

Overstitch

Blanket stitch: This looks better if it is worked upside down, so that the runs between the stitches are under the border rather than on the top edge. Start in the same manner as for overstitch by bringing a length of thread through to the outside of the basket under the binding strips. Then take it to the right, to the point where the next stitch is to be made, and thread it back through to the inside under the binding. Bring the thread up over the top of the binding, down the outside, and under the stitch on the outside. Pull it tight and then repeat the process.

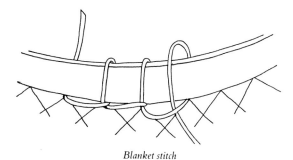

Blanket stitch

Knotted blanket stitch: This is very attractive but takes quite a lot longer to do than the previous two stitches. Start in the same manner as for blanket stitch, bringing the end through to the outside, taking it along to the point where the next stitch is to be made and threading it back through to the inside. Bring the end up over the top of the binding and down over the stitch which is under the binding. Take it up under the stitch to the left, over itself, and down through the stitch to the right. The end is then taken along to the next point where a stitch is to be made and the whole process is repeated. This stitch needs to be kept tight as it is worked because it is difficult to tighten once the knot is in place.

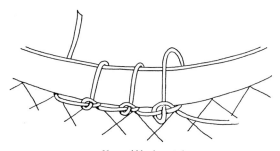

Knotted blanket stitch

Right: *Painted card wastepaper basket with bound border; height c. 30 cm (12 in)*

Far right: *Painted card clutch bag with woven border; width c. 26 cm (10¼ in)*

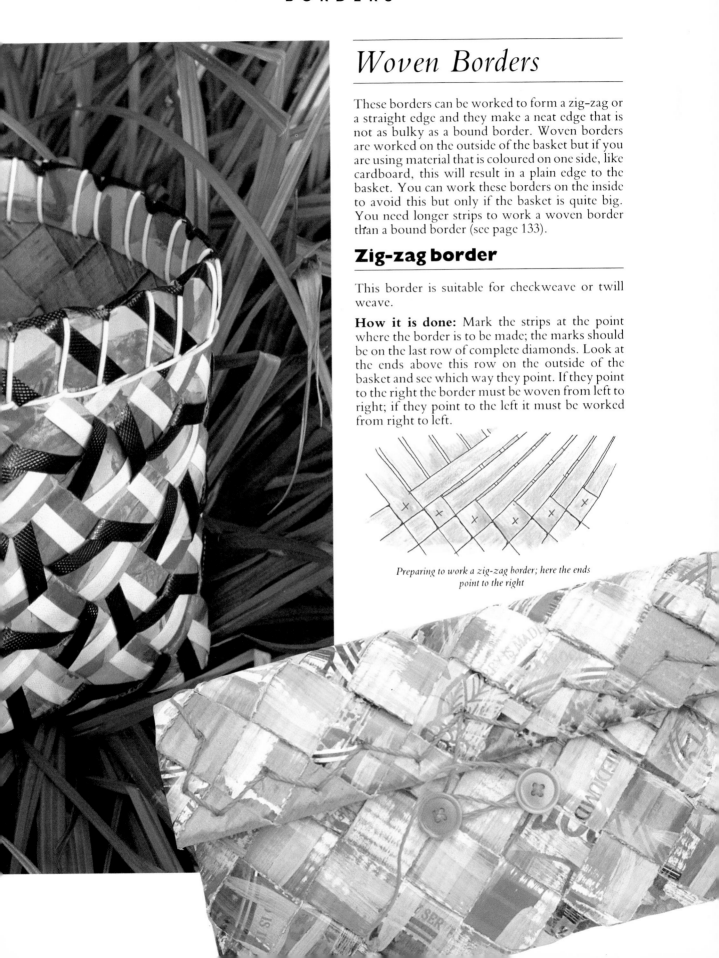

Woven Borders

These borders can be worked to form a zig–zag or a straight edge and they make a neat edge that is not as bulky as a bound border. Woven borders are worked on the outside of the basket but if you are using material that is coloured on one side, like cardboard, this will result in a plain edge to the basket. You can work these borders on the inside to avoid this but only if the basket is quite big. You need longer strips to work a woven border than a bound border (see page 133).

Zig-zag border

This border is suitable for checkweave or twill weave.

How it is done: Mark the strips at the point where the border is to be made; the marks should be on the last row of complete diamonds. Look at the ends above this row on the outside of the basket and see which way they point. If they point to the right the border must be woven from left to right; if they point to the left it must be worked from right to left.

Preparing to work a zig-zag border; here the ends point to the right

Start by taking one of these free ends and folding it back on itself, down to the outside. Then fold the strip that it crosses back on itself and over the one you have just folded. Take the next free end and repeat the process. Work all the way round the basket like this. Then cut the free ends which are now on top on the outside to a point and thread them into the weaving on the outside of the basket, under the diamond immediately below a point on the edge. Any ends left sticking out can be trimmed closely, although if they are very long another border can be worked with them.

work another border, either the zig-zag type or an additional straight edge one. Another option is to cut the ends to make a decorative edge.

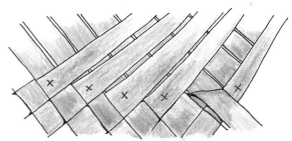

First stage of a straight edge border

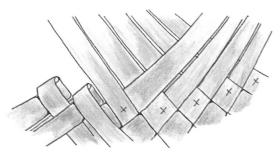

Folding the strips all the way around

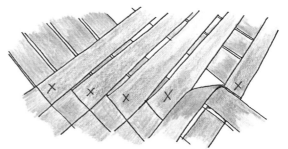

Second stage of a straight edge border

Finishing a zig-zag border

Straight edge border

This is slightly more difficult to do than a zig-zag border but it creates an attractive and strong edge.

How it is done: Mark the strips at the point where the border is to be. Look at the direction in which the ends on the outside of the basket are pointing. If they point to the right you must work the border from right to left, and vice versa. Fold a marked strip towards you so that the fold runs horizontally across the diamond. Take the strip behind it and fold that as well in the same place; this will point the other way. Repeat the process with the next marked strip, taking it over the last strip you folded forwards. Cut a point on the end and thread it into the diamond lying in the V between the first pair of folded ends. Then fold the end at the back forwards.

Continue in this manner, threading the marked end and folding the other. The ends left sticking out should all be trimmed carefully. Alternatively, if there is a lot of material left you could

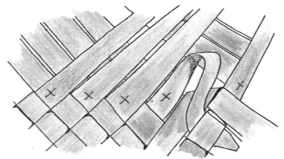

Third stage of a straight edge border

Completed straight edge border

Right: *Cross pattern*

Surface Decoration

After you have made the basket you can enhance it further with additional decoration threaded into the layers of weave. In the case of baskets with bound borders it is usually easier to add this before working the border. Many different materials can be used to work this extra layer, but bear in mind that it will be the outermost layer on the basket and therefore will be subjected to the most wear. If, for example, you choose a pattern with long unwoven runs, do not use a material that will tear or break if it catches on something.

Some of the materials that I use are polypropylene tape, chair cane, flat-band cane, plastic cane, plastic tubing and computer tape. When considering the colour to use I generally choose one that either already features in the basket or is complementary to the other colours.

Threaded-through Pattern

This is a very simple pattern which accentuates the diagonal nature of the weaving on the basket.

How it is done: Simply thread your material – I usually use a flat material such as tape or cane – through on top of the weavers.

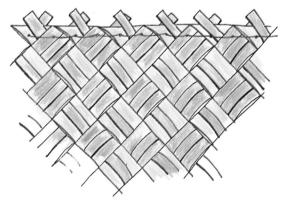

Threaded-through pattern

Cross Pattern

As the name implies, this pattern creates crosses.

How it is done: Starting at the border, thread the decorating weaver under a strip and diagonally over two adjacent strips, so that it then goes under a strip on the next row. Continue like this. You will find as you work across the base of the basket and up the other side that the angle of the pattern will turn at right angles to the decorating weavers on the first side. As you add more weavers they will start to form crosses.

First stage of cross pattern

138

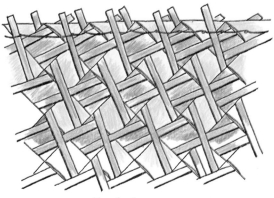

Completed cross pattern

Different patterns can be created depending on whether you start a weaver on every strip or every so many.

Crosses and Dashes Pattern

For this pattern to work you need to have a number of diamonds around the border that divides by three.

How it is done: Start by inserting two weavers on two consecutive strips and then miss out a strip. Continue in this manner all the way round, then work as for cross pattern.

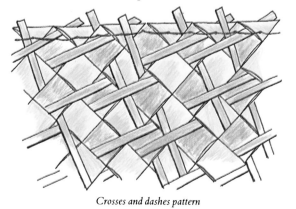

Crosses and dashes pattern

Step Pattern

This creates a very strong surface pattern so the colour you use for this needs to be considered quite carefully.

How it is done: Working from left to right, take a weaver under a strip horizontally. Then take it down vertically over a diamond and under a strip to the right horizontally as before. Continue in this manner. The steps are formed as you work round the basket.

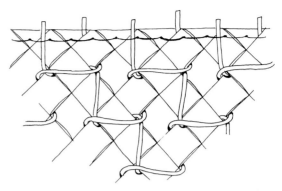

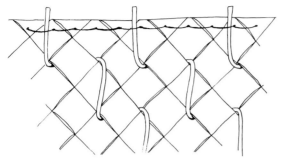

First stage of step pattern

Below: *Step pattern worked with polypropylene tape on painted card*

Second stage of step pattern

All these patterns work on square- and oblong-based baskets, but depending on how many strips were used to make the basket, it is sometimes necessary to work the surface decoration out of sequence on the bases, in order for it to match on all sides of the basket.

Handles

The type of handle you make for a plaited basket will depend on the use to which the basket will be put and the material from which the basket is made.

Cane Baskets

Side handles

The single-rod twisted handle, as described in the stake and strand section (see page 82), is very suitable for small baskets. If an open weave has been used the cane can be threaded through spaces in the weave under the border; on close weaving you can use a bodkin to pierce a hole for the cane.

Alternatively, if the basket is to have a bound border a notched handle can be used. This is prepared before binding the border. Make a handle bow out of handle cane, cutting it long enough to extend below the bound border by 2.5 cm (1 in). Cut a notch 2.5 cm (1 in) from each end and as wide as the binding on the border. Then work the bound border, trapping the handles in place with the notches on the inside of the basket.

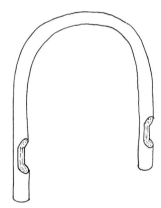

Cane handle with notches cut out

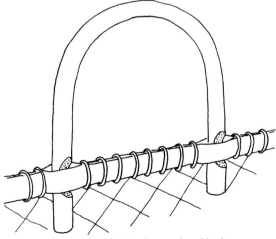

Notched cane handle in place in a bound border

Left: Rope and eyelet handles on a painted card basket

Cross handles

A notched handle can also be used for a cross handle, but if the basket is to get a lot of use then it would probably be advisable to use two bows and to wrap them as well. For additional strengthening, a split pin could be inserted into a small hole drilled through the handle and the border of the basket.

Cords and ropes are easy to attach to a cane basket and make good handles for shoulder bags. These can be threaded through the weaving or the border and knotted or bound to form a loop. Alternatively, a cane ring (see page 85) or metal ring can be worked into the basket as it is being woven and the cord threaded through that.

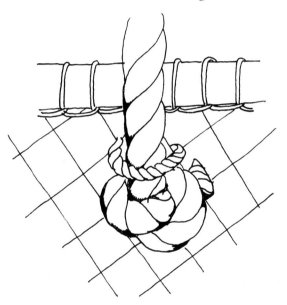

Rope handle threaded through a loop on the outside of a basket

Cardboard Baskets

Side handles

All the methods suitable for cane are also suitable for cardboard, with the addition of materials that can be stapled or riveted on, such as leather or polypropylene tapes.

Cross handles

Again, the same methods as for cane are suitable, but for bags to carry my personal preference is for rope handles threaded through eyelets. These are simple, strong and colourful.

141

Finishing Touches

Lids

In plaited work there are three main types of lid: the drop-over lid, the drop-on lid, and the flap lid.

Drop-over lids

These are made in the same manner as the basket but are woven either a little looser or with more strips. The method you use will depend to a certain extent on the type of borders you use on the basket and lid. For example, bound borders are quite bulky so you would probably need to use more strips on the lid to allow for this.

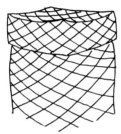

Drop-over lid

Drop-on lids

These are flat lids exactly the same diameter or slightly bigger than the basket and are held in place by a locating rim made out of heavy cane or cardboard attached inside the lid. If you have stitched the border on the lid, a cane rim can be stitched to the underside of the border stitching, provided the position of the stitches is appropriate. Alternatively, a strip of card folded lengthwise and stitched in place makes a sturdy rim. The locating rim needs to be positioned so that it will sit about 1 cm (⅜ in) inside the inner edge of the border. If it is not possible to use the border stitching, new stitching will need to be made. In this case you will need to consider what effect this will have on the appearance of the lid and use appropriately coloured material to stitch with.

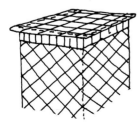

Drop-on lid

Left: *Painted card clutch bag with flap lid; width c. 24 cm (9½ in)*

Flap lids

Flap lids are most commonly found on items like satchels and clutch bags. A flap lid is basically an extension of the back of the basket which folds forwards over the opening and is fastened on the front, using straps and buckles, a toggle and eyelet (US equivalent: button and loop) type of fastening, or a snap fastener. Flap lids can most easily be made square or pointed in shape, although any shape can be used if you employ a bound border.

To create the flap, the basket is bordered at the front and sides but the back is woven further to obtain a piece long enough to reach over to the front. You will need to add extra weavers to do this.

An alternative way of making a flap lid is to weave a separate piece and stitch it onto the back of the basket.

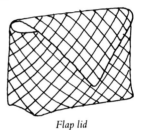

Flap lid

Creasing

You will find that a plaited basket seems to want to turn itself into a ball, even if it has corners. To make the base square so that it will sit flat you need to crease it along its outline. This is particularly necessary with cardboard.

How it is done: With one hand inside the basket pushing along the line where the crease is to be made, use the other hand to pinch the material on the outside along the same line. Once the initial crease has been made, you can fold it firmly using both hands on the outside of the basket.

Creasing can also be done up the sides at the corners so that the whole basket takes on a square or rectangular form.

Varnishing

This is particularly essential for plaited cardboard baskets and is done as already described for stake and strand baskets on page 91.

143

Design Calculations

Before you start making your basket you will need to know how many strips to use, how long and wide they should be and, if you are painting cardboard, how much you need to decorate.

Width of strips

The width of the strips is simply a matter of preference, taking into account the scale of the finished piece and the strength required. I find that corrugated card of less than 3 cm (1¼ in) width is more likely to tear as it is worked. I use strips of the same width for most baskets, so that I can use up all the left-overs on another one if I want to.

Length of strips

The calculations for these are slightly different depending on whether the base is square or rectangular.

Square bases: First decide how big you want the final piece to be. To work out how long the strips need to be for a basket with a bound border, add one third extra onto the total measurement down one side, across the bottom, and up the other side of the basket. So, if your finished basket is to be 30 cm (12 in) wide and 30 cm (12 in) high the total measurement of the two sides and the bottom will be 90 cm (36 in). By adding on a third of this you will determine that the length of your strips needs to be 120 cm (48 in).

If you are going to make a basket with a folded border you need to allow extra length, determined by the width of the strips, as indicated below:

Width of strips	Extra to add to each strip
2 cm (¾ in)	12 cm (4¾ in)
3 cm (1¼ in)	16 cm (6¼ in)
4 cm (1½ in)	20 cm (8 in)

Rectangular bases: To make a finished basket 40 cm (15¾ in) long, 10 cm (4 in) wide and 30 cm (12 in) high, for example, add together the length and width, then divide that by 2 to get an average measurement. This will give you 25 cm (9¾ in). Continue your calculations as for a square base, but using 25 cm (9¾ in) as the width. Therefore, the total measurement of the two sides and the bottom will be 85 cm (33¾ in). A third added to this will bring the final measurement for the strips to 113 cm (45 in). Again, this measurement is for baskets with bound borders; if you are working a folded border you will need to allow more, as explained above.

Number of strips

As before, estimate the finished base measurements of your basket. Because the corners of the bases in plaited work are actually formed in the centres of the sides of the woven area, initially you need to weave a bigger area than your finished base. The width of this area is determined by the diagonal measurement of the finished base. This is calculated by using the mathematical formula Pythagoras's Theorem, which states that the square on the hypotenuse is equal to the sum of the squares on the other two sides. If mathematics are not your strong point, however, there is a simpler way to calculate this: draw the outline of your proposed finished base actual size on a piece of paper (newspaper will do) and measure the diagonal.

Once you have established the width of the square area to be woven you can calculate how many strips are needed in each direction by dividing this measurement by the width of the strips. For example, a 30 cm (12 in) square base with a diagonal measuring 42 cm (16½ in) to be woven with strips that are 4 cm (1½ in) wide would need ten or eleven strips in each direction. Unless you particularly want a lopsided border you should use an even number in each direction (as explained on page 124), so choose ten. The total number of strips required is therefore twenty, although if you are working a bound border you will need two extra ones with which to do the binding. The same calculations are used for rectangular bases.

Having worked out how many strips are required, and how long and wide they are to be, it is easy to calculate the amount of cardboard to paint.

Left: *Cone-shaped bowl in painted card; diameter c. 30 cm (12 in)*

Plaiting Projects

Oblong Card Bag with Handles

Strictly speaking, this is a stake and strand basket because it has a base and because extra weavers are added to weave the sides; but as the technique for weaving the cardboard is identical to the other plaited card baskets in this section it seems sensible to include it here. If you intend to use this basket a lot, rope or leather, rather than tape, handles might be better as they are more comfortable to hold.

Finished measurements

Height: 26 cm (10¼ in)
Width: 12.5 cm (5 in)
Length: 37 cm (14½ in)

Materials

9 strips of painted cardboard 70 cm (27½ in) long and 4 cm (1½ in) wide

3 strips of painted cardboard 90 cm (36 in) long and 4 cm (1½ in) wide

8 strips of painted cardboard 120 cm (48 in) long and 4 cm (1½ in) wide

Approximately 20 m (22 yd) of 1 cm (⅜ in) wide polypropylene tape, cane, or similar material for decoration and stitching the top edge

2 lengths of tape or rope 70 cm (27½ in) long for handles

Approximately 2.25 m (2½ yd) of strong stitching thread which will not be visible on the finished basket

Tools

Scissors
Flexible steel tape measure
Large-eyed needle
Small/medium bodkin or awl
Clothes pegs (US: clothespins)
Eyelet hole punch and eyelet punch
Hammer
Stapler

Instructions

Weave an area of *checkweave*, three strips wide and nine strips long, using the 90 cm (36 in) and 70 cm (27½ in) long strips. Bend up the strips around this flat area and then, using the 120 cm (48 in) long strips, weave up six rows. Overlap the ends of the strips and start each row in a different place, trying to work as tightly as possible as you go along. When you have done these six rows, go over the whole piece *tightening* it up so that there are no holes or loops anywhere. Peg round the top and *stitch* along the centre of the top row. Trim the cardboard 1 cm (⅜ in) above the stitching. Decorate with the crosses and dashes pattern.

To make a *bound border*, peg the binding strips in place, one inside and one outside, and, using either a piece of tape cut to half its width or some other card, *blanket stitch* them in place.

If you are using tape for the handles, turn the basket upside down and, starting at the third strip in from the end, thread the tape under the card from the bottom of the basket up to the top edge. Make the handle loop and thread the tape back down the same side, three strips in from the other end. Weave it across the bottom of the basket and up the other side. Make the loop, then work the tape back down to the point where you started. Adjust the handles to the right size, then, holding the two ends of tape together, pull them out towards you sufficiently to be able to staple them together in two or three places. Adjust the tape so that the join is hidden under a strip.

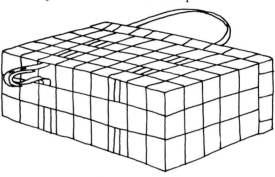

Stapling the handle tape

If you are using leather it can either be worked in the same manner as tape or simply riveted onto the side of the basket. Then *varnish* the basket inside and out. If you want to have rope handles, varnish the basket first then put eyelets into the top edge of the basket and thread the rope through, either knotting it or binding it to make a loop.

Previous page: Oblong card bag with handles

Small Card Tub

I make baskets like this one to use as wastepaper baskets, but with a lid and a carrying strap it would make quite a useful bag.

Finished measurements

Height: 26 cm (10¼ in)
Width: 22 cm (8¾ in)

Materials

14 strips of painted cardboard 102 cm (40 in) long and 4 cm (1½ in) wide
Approximately 20 m (22 yd) of polypropylene cord or similar material for decoration
Approximately 3 m (3¼ yd) of polypropylene or cotton cord or similar material for stitching the top edge (should match the decorative cord in colour)
Approximately 1.5 m (1⅔ yd) of strong stitching thread which will not be visible on the finished basket

Tools

Scissors
Flexible steel tape measure
Large-eyed needle
Small/medium bodkin or awl
Clothes pegs (US: clothespins)

Instructions

Weave an area of *checkweave* measuring six strips by six strips. Make the *corners*, using the central two strips on each side, then weave up the sides until the work measures 26 cm (10¼ in) from them. *Tighten* up everything and peg to hold the work in place. *Stitch* round, starting in the top of the fifth diamond up from a corner. Trim the cardboard 1 cm (⅜ in) above the stitching. Decorate with the *step pattern*, using the cord.

Make a *bound border*, using the two remaining strips. *Blanket stitch* this with the polypropylene or cotton cord. *Crease* the bottom edges of the tub and *varnish* inside and out.

Right: *Small card tub*

Card Shoulder Bag

This bag has very long handles so that it can be carried across the body as well as over the shoulder, but you can of course make the handles any length you like. You can also make the bag bigger or smaller by increasing or decreasing the number of strips you use, but remember that you must work with an even number. Any of the surface decoration patterns can be used.

Finished measurements

Height: 26 cm (10¼ in)
Width: 20 cm (8 in)
Length: 38 cm (15 in)

Materials

18 strips of painted cardboard 100 cm (39½ in) long and 4 cm (1½ in) wide
16 m (17½ yd) of 1 cm (⅜ in) wide polypropylene tape or flat–band cane for decoration
Approximately 4 m (4⅓ yd) of tape, chair cane, cord or other material for stitching round the top
Approximately 2 m (2¼ yd) of strong stitching thread which will not be visible on the finished basket
4 15 mm (⅝ in) eyelets
2.5 m (2¾ yd) of 12 mm (½ in) polypropylene rope or cord for the handles
4 m (4⅓ yd) of fine polycord or other strong cord to bind the handles
8 beads with holes large enough to take the binding cord

Tools

Scissors
Flexible steel tape measure
Large-eyed needle
Small/medium bodkin or awl
Clothes pegs (US: clothespins)
Eyelet hole punch and eyelet punch
Hammer

Instructions

Weave an area of *checkweave* measuring eight strips by eight strips. Make the four *corners*, using the second and third strips away from two diagonally opposite corners of the square. Weave up the sides until the work measures 25 cm (9¾ in) from the corners. *Tighten up* everything and peg to hold in place. *Stitch* round, starting from the bottom of the fifth diamond up from a corner. Trim the

cardboard 1 cm (⅜ in) above the stitching. *Crease the bottom edges and the corners of the basket, then decorate with the tape or cane, using the threaded-through pattern*. Peg the binding strips on, one inside and one outside, and, using a length of tape cut to half its width (or cord), stitch them in place with *blanket stitch*.

Mark with a pencil where the eyelets are to go and then pull out any tape or cane under the mark, so that it does not get split when the eyelet is made. Place a block of wood under the edge of the basket and make the holes with the eyelet hole punch and hammer. Put in the eyelets and hammer into place with the eyelet punch. Thread the handle rope through to the desired length. If you are using polypropylene rope, cut it with a sharp knife and melt the ends with a flame – a lighter will do, but preferably use a blue flame or the melted part of the rope will turn black. Bring the short end up 6 cm (2½ in) inside the basket.

Tie a knot in the end of your binding cord and thread a bead onto it. Thread the cord into the needle and stitch through the centre of the double thickness of handle rope and down as close to the top edge of the basket as possible. Wrap tightly twelve times, then stitch through from back to front and thread another bead on. Knot the end of the cord tightly. Repeat this procedure on the other three handle ends. If you are using polycord, melt the ends of the cord at the knots very carefully to seal them. Finally, *varnish* the bag inside and out with at least two coats.

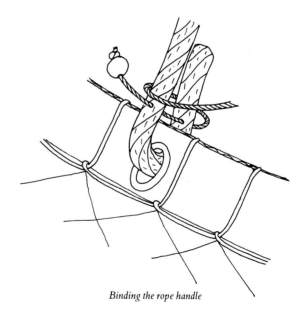

Binding the rope handle

Left: *Card shoulder bag*

151

Diamond-shaped Card Tray

Although I have called this a tray it will serve equally well as a dish, in which case it would not be necessary to make the handles. If you want to use it as a tray I recommend at least three coats of varnish inside and out to make sure it is stiff enough. You will also need to turn the tray upside down and weight it slightly in the middle during the last stages of drying to make sure that it sits flat.

Finished measurements

Height excluding handles: 6 cm (2½ in)
Width: 39 cm (15½ in)
Length excluding handles: 56 cm (22 in)

Materials

14 strips of painted cardboard 60 cm (23¾ in) long and 4 cm (1½ in) wide
10 strips of painted cardboard 76 cm (30 in) long and 4 cm (1½ in) wide
1 strip of painted cardboard 150 cm (59 in) long and 4 cm (1½ in) wide, *or* two additional 76 cm (30 in) long strips, for the border
Approximately 4.5 m (5 yd) of plastic cane, cord, tape or similar material for stitching the top edge
Approximately 10 m (11 yd) of 1 cm (⅜ in) wide polypropylene tape or flat-band cane for the step pattern and handles
Approximately 4.5 m (5 yd) of 5 mm (³⁄₁₆ in) wide polypropylene tape or flat-band cane for the threaded-through pattern
Approximately 3 m (3¼ yd) of strong stitching thread which will not be visible on the finished tray

Tools

Scissors
Rigid steel rule
Large-eyed needle
Small/medium bodkin or awl
Clothes pegs (US: clothespins)

Instructions

Weave a rectangle of *checkweave*, using the ten long strips across the fourteen short strips, and peg to hold. On the undecorated side of the card and using a rigid rule, draw a line from the centre of each side of the weaving to the centre of the adjacent side. This will mark a diamond and will be the line along which the work will be creased to form the edges.

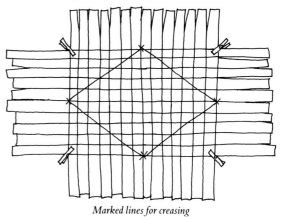

Marked lines for creasing

Make the four *corners*, using the two central strips on each side. Weave as much as is necessary to hold the shape then peg securely. *Crease* firmly along the marked lines, *tighten up* everything, and peg to hold.

It is now necessary to mark where the stitching will go. Because the length is greater than the width it is not possible to use the weave as a guideline as you can with a square- or rectangular-based basket. Draw a line 5 cm (2 in) up and parallel with the crease line on the outside of the tray. *Stitch* around on this line. Trim the card 1 cm (3/8 in) above the stitching.

Decorate every other row of weaving with the *step pattern*, using the 1 cm (3/8 in) wide tape or cane. Then work the *threaded-through pattern*, using the 5 mm (3/16 in) wide tape or cane, so that it crosses over the already worked pattern. Trim any excess tape or cane level with the top edge of the tray.

To *bind* the top edge, take the remaining long strip of card and fold it lengthways. *Blanket stitch* this in place, using the plastic cane.

To make the *handles*, cut two 80 cm (31½ in) lengths of the 1 cm (3/8 in) wide tape or cane. Take one piece and thread one end under the stitching on the outside approximately 6 cm (2½ in) from the point at one end of the tray. Form the loop that will be the handle and thread the other end of the tape or cane under the stitching approximately 12 cm (4¾ in) away on the other side of the point.

Left: Diamond-shaped card tray

153

Adjust the loop to the right height for your hands to hold the tray by, and then take the tape or cane back and forth in the same manner until there are four layers of it. Repeat at the other end of the tray.

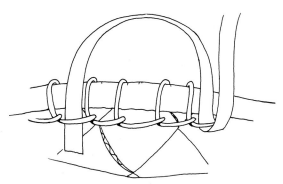

Starting to make the handle

To pierce the tape for the decoration, which will also hold the handle together, heat a bodkin in a gas flame or on an electric ring and when it is very hot push it through the layers of tape at regular intervals. Using a piece of the narrow tape split in half lengthways, thread it in and out of the holes and cut the ends off flush with the base of the handles.

To finish the basket, apply at least three coats of *varnish*.

Right: *Cane purse*

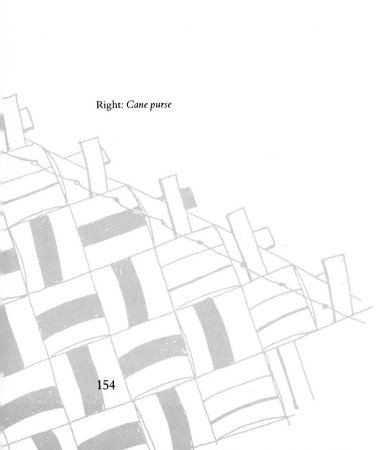

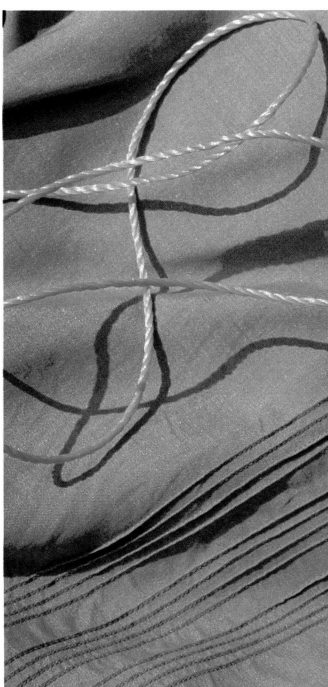

Cane Purse

I enjoyed making this purse a lot. The finished article is light and strong. The same principles could also be applied to make a much bigger shoulder bag, or perhaps a longer case for glasses or pencils, or even a wider version for a camera.

Finished measurements

Height: 10 cm (4 in)
Width of bottom section: 4 cm (1½ in)
Width of lid: 5 cm (2 in)
Length of bottom section: 8 cm (3⅛ in)
Length of lid: 9.5 cm (3¾ in)

Materials

Dyed lapping or flat-band cane 5 mm (³⁄₁₆ in) wide in orange, turquoise and royal blue:
    20 pieces 35 cm (13¾ in) long for bottom section
    2 pieces 25 cm (9¾ in) long for binding bottom section
    24 pieces 18 cm (7 in) long for the lid
    2 pieces 27 cm (10⅝ in) long for binding the lid
2.25 m (2½ yd) of fine strong cord for stitching
110 cm (43¼ in) of cord

Tools

Side-cutters or secateurs
Piece of willow or cane or small screwdriver (to push the canes close together)
Clothes pegs (US: clothespins)
Large-eyed needle
Stapler
Flexible steel tape measure

Instructions

To make the bottom section, weave a *twill weave* rectangular base using ten damped canes in each direction. Push the work up as tightly as possible and make sure the woven area is square. Peg to hold in place. Make the *corners* with the third and fourth canes away from the two diagonal corners (which will be indicated by the pattern). Making the corners is tricky on this scale so keep the work well pegged all the time. Weave ten rows of twill weave and then *tighten up* everything.

Staple round the basket on a line with the tenth row and then trim the canes carefully, immediately above the staples in a straight line. Add more staples if necessary. Take the binding strips and damp them and the top edge of the basket so that the canes will not split unduly when stitched through. With one binding strip inside and one outside, covering the staples and the cut ends of the cane, *blanket stitch* in position tightly.

The *lid* is worked in exactly the same manner but using twenty-four strips, twelve in each direction and with only four rows of weaving. Prior to stapling the top edge, check that the lid fits snugly on the bottom section, allowing for the binding. Then work the *bound border*.

The neck cord is threaded through gaps in the weaving on the lid and the ends are then threaded down through the border of the bottom section and knotted inside. The lid slides up and down.

Suppliers of Materials and Tools

Tint & Splint Basketry, Inc.   *Dyed reed, classes*
30100 Ford Road
Garden City, MI 48135
(313) 522-7760

Royalwood Ltd.
517 Woodville Road
Mansfield, OH 44907
(419) 526-1630

Gundula's Chair Caning and
    Basket Weaving
1300 Goodwin Avenue
Springfield, OH 45504
(513) 323-5062

Earth Guild   *Dyes*
One Tingle Alley
Asheville, NC 28801
(704) 255-7818

Basket Beginnings   *Exotics*
P.O. Box 24815
San Jose, CA 95154-4815
(408) 269-4513

English Basketry Willows   *Willow and its*
Rural Free Delivery 1,   *paraphernalia only*
    Box 124A
South New Berlin,
    NY 13843-9649
(607) 847-8264

Connecticut Cane and Reed
    Company
Box 762P
Manchester, CT 06040

Basket and Caning Cottage
906 Park Avenue #5
Orange Park, FL 32073
(904) 264-9609

Country Seat   *Basket making and chair*
Box 24-RD#2   *seating*
Kempton, PA 19529-9411
(215) 756-6124

Ozark Basketry Supply   *All basket supplies*
P.O. Box 56-C.B.
Kingston, AR 72742
(501) 665-2702

Hole punches, eyelets and eyelet punches are to be found in craft stores.

Packaging tapes (polypropylene) can be bought in very large quantities from most firms specializing in packaging materials. Small quantities can be easily gathered in towns or saved for you by your local supermarket if you ask nicely.

Bibliography

This is a list of books on basket making that I have particularly enjoyed and found useful:

Butcher, Mary, *Willow Work*, Dryad Press, 1986
Duchesne, R., *La Vannerie*, Vol. I, J. B. Bailliere et Fils, 1963
Japanese Bamboo Baskets, 'Form and Function' series,
    Kodansha Press, 1980
La Plantz, Shereen, *Plaited Basketry: The Woven Form*, Press
    de la Plantz, 1982
Lane, Robert F., *Philippine Basketry: An Appreciation*,
    Bookmark Inc., 1986
Okey, Thomas, *An Introduction to the Art of Basketmaking*,
    Pitman, 1932, reprinted by Dryad Press, 1987
Will, Christoph, *Die Korbflechterei*, Verlag Georg D. W.,
    1978
Wright, Dorothy, *The Complete Book of Baskets and Basketry*,
    David & Charles, 1977, reprinted 1983

Index

INDEX